2691CB00004B/6

CARTONQTY:BLACKSTD PERFECT

2691CBX00015B - 2691CBX00017B [3 : 434]

*** 2 6 9 1 C B 0 0 0 0 4 B ***

**

TAT**

BOOK
STBW19_SM   CONTAINS: MONO

Department   Operator's Name (Please print)

Printing   ___________________________________

Binding   ___________________________________

Cutting   ___________________________________

Shipping   ___________________________________

Batch Location   ___________________________________

Promise Date: 20-DEC-23 (WED)

Printed at: Tue Dec 19 16:47:10 2023 on device cbhp02-50

Batch 2691CB00004B

2691CBX00015B	9781955791786	Awaken the Excellence in Your Child		
PERFECT	6.00X9.00	168	GLOSS	(205)
2691CBX00016B	9781734315363	Young Boss: Your Youth is Your Power		
PERFECT	6.00X9.00	148	GLOSS	(104)
2691CBX00017B	9781732451162	25 Servings of SOOP: Literary Journeys		
PERFECT	6.00X9.00	142	GLOSS	(125)

Printed in the USA
CPSIA information can be obtained
at www.ICGtesting.com
CBHW021648191223
2691CB00004B

AWAKEN THE Excellence IN YOUR CHILD

Printed in the United States of America

First Printing, 2023

Softcover ISBN 978-1-955791-78-6
Hardcover ISBN 978-1-955791-89-2

Library of Congress Control Number: 2023918404

Ordering Information: Special discounts are available on quantity purchases by bookstores, corporations, associations, and others. For details, contact the publisher at sales@ braughlerbooks.com or at 937-58-BOOKS.

For questions or comments about this book, please write to info@braughlerbooks.com.

Braughler
Books
braughlerbooks.com

To my wonderful children of excellence.

You are a gift from God, and I am honored to be your mom.

Contents

Introduction 1

Principle #1: Live by example

Chapter 1 Training the Trainer 7

Principle #2: Take control of your emotions

Chapter 2 Check Your Pride at the Door! 17

Chapter 3 I Can't Hear You…
Because Your Voice Is Too Loud! 25

Principle #3: Understand the power of your words

Chapter 4 Two Negatives Don't Equal a Positive 33

Chapter 5 Use Your Words…Wisely 39

Chapter 6 "Put-Me-Downs" 47

Principle #4: Focus on Character not Rules

Chapter 7 Rule #1: Quit Having So Many Rules! 57

Chapter 8 Training Through the Power of a Question ... 65

Principle #5: Pray more, talk less

Chapter 9 Pray Without Ceasing: The Prayer 79

Principle #6: Build an environment that produces excellence

Chapter 10	A Lesson Learned from Popeye	89
Chapter 11	Let It Rain	97
Chapter 12	10 Million Dollar Baby	103
Chapter 13	Go Team Go!	115

Principle #7: Develop your Preamble

Chapter 14	Raising Your Child "On Purpose": The Preamble	125

Principle #8: Beware of controlling relationships

Chapter 15	Bon Appétit!	137
Chapter 16	Relationships	147

Principles	157
Foundational Verses	159

Introduction

I have a confession.... I used to be very judgmental of parents of unruly children. But that was during my BC (*Before Children*) days. I would see these kids in the grocery store or the malls, acting as if they had just lost their minds, and I would say, "Boy, when I have children, they are not going to act like that!" or "Why don't those parents get control of their kid?" But *after* I had children, you know the song that goes, "*I pray for you, you pray for me...*"? Let's just say that became my theme song.[1]

That overwhelming feeling prompted me to pray for God's help. I needed God to disciple me in raising my children because I knew I didn't have the patience. Left to my own devices, I would *surely* mess it up! Now you may think I prayed this prayer after I failed in some area while raising my children. But no! I prayed this prayer before I was married and before I had my first child. I saw how defeated the parents looked and how relentless their children were, and, honestly, it scared me. What if my children turned out to be little monsters?!

Seriously, the truth of the matter is just because your child decides to "act up" in public does not mean

<hr>

1 "I Need You to Survive" by Hezekiah Walker.

you're a bad parent or you are not trying to exercise good parenting skills. *Special note to parents who have preschoolers*: Handling public temper tantrums is easy when compared to dealing with teen peer pressures, trust, dating, and self-esteem issues. But don't lose hope!

My life isn't the stereotypical perfect scenario with an ideal marriage, two children, a dog, and a house with a white picket fence! I'm a divorced, single parent who worked two jobs and still had financial struggles. And I raised three independent, non-judgmental, God-fearing adults who make good decisions and contribute positively to society.

Now before you think it, I will set the record straight. I am not an exception to the rule, as all three of my children are quite different in personalities, interests, and temperaments. So, I know firsthand the frustrations of dealing with temper tantrums, running away from home, depression, discipline tactics that have no impact...and more. On top of that, add problems that arise from going through a divorce. But I also know the great elation of raising children who realize their potential and achieve excellence despite obstacles! God answered my prayers and regularly gave me what I called golden principles for raising my children. I call them principles intentionally because a principle is not germane to my situation only; it's a foundational truth that is valid for whoever puts it into practice. And that is what I will share with you.

These life lessons are very personal, but I want to be transparent. Reason being, I'm always amazed when people ask me how is it that I, as a single parent, raised all three of my children to such a level of excellence? They are all responsible, respectful, ambitious visionaries who have multiple degrees, travel the world, avidly volunteer, and are regularly being honored for outstanding performance and contributions.

Before I go on, let me say a resounding THANK YOU GOD!! But it's not that my children are *Super Kids*...well, actually they are...to me...but they are not perfect! However, they possess excellence, as does your child, and we as parents have the awesome opportunity to awaken their excellence so they can reach their potential.

I heard a wonderful message from a pastor[2] who said that "parent" means to *bring forth.* I love that! We, through parenting, have the awesome privilege to bring forth the excellence in our children. But unfortunately, that works both ways. There were many times that I brought forth the worse, as you will read about in later chapters of my book.

Before we start this journey, I pray you will let down your guard and allow God to speak to you without judging yourself. As I have shared, and will continue to share throughout this book, I didn't have it all together. But because you've chosen to read this book, you've started the awakening journey. Take some time now to surrender your thoughts, beliefs, emotions, and will to God so He can perfect what He has started (Philippians 1:6, NIV). I believe what you demonstrate and speak over your children will awaken that quality in them, and I am committed to walking with you as

---

2 Pastor Steven Furtick, Jr., Elevation Church. Charlotte, NC.

a guide so you can ***Awaken the Excellence in Your Child***.

Here's how this will work. At the end of each chapter, I suggest one or two ideas for you to "Put into Practice." I have shared these principles and lessons with other parents, and they have been life changing. My hope is that this will be a life-changing experience for you as well. Come take this journey with me and

Awaken the Excellence in Your Child!

Principle #1:

Live by example

Chapter 1

Training the Trainer

I have not been—and I believe it's safe to say, I shall never be—the "perfect parent." Parenting involves a lot of training. Wouldn't you agree? From day one, we're training our little ones to sit up, roll over, crawl, eat solid foods, walk, talk, go to the potty…and the list goes on and on! We as parents are supposed to know instinctively the best way to train our children, and it's for certain that if we do not, some well-meaning person will criticize us into thinking that something is either wrong with us or, worse yet, with our child. Well, let me take the pressure off right now and say: There are no perfect parents. As you will read throughout this book, I blew it many times. However, you will not find another person on this earth who beat me in trying to get it right. As I stated in my introduction, I prayed and asked God to disciple me as I raised my children. My husband's job transferred us frequently, so our first two children were born in a different state than where my family was. I knew I needed practical application and visual support of what good parenting looked like in my day-to-day. That prayer was answered through practical principles that I used as foundational practices in raising my children to a level of excellence…not perfection, but excellence…the utilization of their gifts, strengths, and talents that leads to a life of purpose.

Before I dive deeper into what I mean by training the trainer, let me first clarify. In 1970, the psychologist Abraham Maslow conducted a study on the learning process of humans. He called it Train the Trainer. It is a training framework where leaders in their organizations are taught a new concept while simultaneously learning how to teach it to someone else. This has proven to be very effective because the person learning the new concept is focusing not only on understanding but also on duplication. Maslow's Train the Trainer model is still used by many businesses today.[3]

While this is a wonderful concept, what I am referring to in this chapter on training the trainer is slightly different. I want to build you up so that you will have principles and practices to put in place as you train your child. I am not looking for you to replicate every single thing I did. Your family dynamics may differ greatly from mine; therefore, it would not be best for you to instruct exactly as I instruct. Besides, no two children are the same. However, these principles are transferable and adaptable. They will get you to the end goal, which is obtaining excellence!

I am so excited about us taking this journey together! So, let's take the first step to awakening the excellence in your child, which is to **Awaken the Trainer in You**! Do you view yourself as a trainer? Well, you are. You are your child's personal coach. When I

---

3 https://work.chron.com/train-trainer-model-5463.html.

was in junior high and high school, I experienced many coaches. I had cheerleading, drill team, choir, debate team, and several track coaches. But one coach in particular stood out above the rest. She was my favorite. She came from a family of athletes, and they were all known for their skill and many achievements. When this coach gave instructions on how an exceptional athlete must live a life of discipline, I did not question it because I knew it was more than just talk; she walked the walk. When I messed up or was unsure, she was able to do more than explain using her words; she was able to demonstrate the proper technique. She wasn't perfect, but she believed in what she was sharing with me, and it was visible in how she lived her life.

This got me to thinking about my role as a coach to my children. I noticed that my children more easily patterned after what I demonstrated than what I instructed. When you think about it, it doesn't take a rocket scientist to figure this out. This is one of the main reasons that YouTube tutorials are so popular. We tend to relate to and reproduce behaviors if we have a visual example. But even before YouTube, if we wanted to get our point across, we would *paint a picture*. Why? Because we duplicate what we see. Please do not underestimate the power of visualization. Today, we practice visualization through creating vision boards, which are powerful tools that allow us to "see" a better life. Professional athletes even spend hours visualizing the perfecting of their skills. Our children are no exception. Consider the example of your everyday life as a vision board for your child. But much of the time, we do the opposite. We try to live out our unfulfilled dreams through the lives of our children.

If we wanted to be the head cheerleader, the first chair violinist, or the captain of the football team, we push our child to be. But I want to challenge you to do something a little different.

Instead of pushing your child to be the person you wanted to become, why not do the opposite?

YOU be the person you want your child to become.

If you tell your child to make up the bed every morning but they see your bed unmade, chances are you're setting yourself up for many battles—and not just battles over making the bed. Change your practice, or you will soon find yourself having to fight the battle of hypocrisy with your child. Since making the bed is so important for *them* to do, *you* must live that out in your life also. If you're going to talk the talk, then walk the walk because, believe you me, your child will pick up on your inconsistencies. This "Do as I say, not as I do" lifestyle breaks down in other areas too and drives a wedge between you and your child's communication and trust. So, I had to embrace the old adage: Actions speak louder than words. I realized I also needed some training. One verse I heard growing up that all the good bible teachers used comes from Proverbs 22:6 (NIV):

Train a child in the way
he should go, and when he is
old, he will not turn from it.

This is one of the foundational truths I used in raising my children and the first principle I used in awakening their excellence. However, when I hear parents quoting this verse to imply that their wayward child will eventually get back on the right track because they took them to church when they were little, I cringe. Only taking a child to church on Sundays is not abiding by this verse. Let's use common sense here: If all a child sees is "good" on Sunday but "bad" from Monday through Saturday, guess what path they will *tend* to follow? If you answered that question with the "good" path, I want you to close this book right now because you're just not teachable! Just kidding... everyone deserves a second chance. Look at the verse again. Who is the author talking to? King Solomon is sharing proverbs or wise Instructions for us to live by as individuals. He is saying: It is **your** responsibility to train your child, not just the church's responsibility. Yes, the church plays a vital role; it is one of the avenues used in training. However, the command was given to **you**. If you want your child to be kind, **you** should daily exercise kindness. If you want your child to be honest, **you** should daily exercise honesty.

I've read countless books and magazine articles, listened to tapes (yes, tapes, back in the day when we listened to cassette tapes), and attended seminars on Child Rearing, but everyone seemed to focus more on the *trainee* (the child) and less on the *trainer* (the parent). Why is that? It may be because it's easier for the parent to say "Do as I say, not as I do" when instructing their child. I admit it is catchy to develop a "10-step program to developing a disciplined life in your child" if the child is the only one making all the changes. Then if it fails, you can just blame the child…. But that's ridiculous. I've experienced the opposite to be true. When I asked God how do I "train a child," the answer was simple… train yourself and the child will follow.

There's a verse in the Bible inspirationally written by the Apostle Paul to the church in Philippi: "Keep putting into practice all you learned and received from me—everything you heard from me and saw me doing. Then the God of peace will be with you" (Philippians 4:9 NLT). This was another foundational verse that I had in raising my children. My responsibility as the parent was to teach my children through three avenues: written word (received), verbal instruction (heard), and living a life of example (saw me doing). As challenging as this sounds, living out this verse in front of my children was not my greatest struggle. The utmost battle came as I struggled through living out this verse when I was *not* in front of my children. You see, the Apostle Paul had a heart committed to truth. The truth he shared through his epistles concerning conduct and conviction was truth, regardless of the circumstance. If he taught it, then he lived it… because it was truth! So, I had to go back and re-visit some of my lifestyle decisions and discipline, or train, myself so that my life would be an epistle that my children could not only read but also see. Please understand that I am not saying that parents must be blameless before they "train up their child." If that were the case, I would not be in a position to teach anything! But what I am saying is this: Just like the Apostle Paul—who when he wanted to do good, evil was always present[4]—I learned to rely on God's Spirit to empower and sustain me. By doing this, I was also setting an example for my children and teaching them how to navigate through the struggles in life. So, the bottom line is: The more I worked on living as an example, the better the results were in my children.

I want to warn you about two points in particular. First, please do not get caught up in the results. You may not see an instant change in your children, but "do not grow weary in well doing" (Galatians 6:9 KJV). Continue to live the life you want them to pattern after, and the reward will come eventually. Second, do not be caught up in putting yourself down when you fail. Notice that I did not say *if* you fail, but I said **when** you fail because we all have moments where we do not live up to our expectations. So, don't be too hard on yourself. I used to say every morning when I woke up, "God, thank You for another day, and thank You for another opportunity to try to get this right." Forgiveness is the first cousin to resilience: The faster you forgive and move on, the faster you snap back from a setback.

4 Romans 7:21.

PUT INTO PRACTICE

Here's the first task I want you to "Put Into Practice." I want you to examine yourself honestly. What are the weaknesses in your character that prevent you from awakening *your* excellence? Examine yourself. Recognize areas that need work in your own life. If the opportunity arises, instead of fussing with your child about something that you have not mastered, be transparent enough to say so. Let your child know you struggle in that area as well, so the two of you can work on it together. You can, together, set small goals to which you can hold each other accountable. But remember, even if you are working on areas of weakness in your life, don't do all the talking! Let your child have input on how you can take baby steps of improvement.

Now, if you have multiple children, like me, do not be tempted to do a group exercise. No, this should be a one-on-one conversation, where you are sharing your area of weakness and asking them to support you through it. Work with one child and see how that goes before sharing in this exercise with your other children. Believe me, your children are watching and remembering how you handle problems and struggles. Your behavior, whether good or bad, is the biggest influencer in your child's life.

Take baby steps in your training. Building discipline takes consistency. It is a war that is won through small victories.

Principle #2:

Take control of your emotions

Chapter 2

Check Your Pride at the Door!

I hope you will "Put Into Practice" sharing your weaknesses with your child, as discussed in the previous chapter. Pride sometimes stops us from allowing others, especially our children, to see our inadequacies. Maybe it is because we struggle with low self-esteem, but it comes out in prideful words or actions. Or maybe we feel we will lose their respect when they learn we have struggles, but you will come to find the opposite to be true. Your transparency can draw you and your child closer.

Now let's move on to the next lesson God taught me when raising my children. This lesson once again focuses on the Trainer (the parent). I have three children: two girls and a boy. I recall one day, my baby girl and I were having a disagreement (note: you will NEVER hear me refer to her as the "middle child"—I will discuss why later on in the book). Anyway, we were having an intense but respectful discussion, and as she was stating her views and opinions, I found myself getting angry because she was exposing inconsistencies in **my** character. Now, I could have pulled the *Mommy card* and said, "Look, little one, I don't care what you think. This is what I said! Now go to your room!" But this time, I didn't.

Sometimes the area that we battle the most with our child is the same area we need the most work in ourselves.

So, I got my emotions (pride) in check and tried to **listen** to what she was saying. Readers: I hope you got that: I had to check myself. My instinctive attitude was: How could this child I birthed correct me?! Now Old School would say, "Don't she know that I brought her into this world, and I will take her out!" But the truth of the matter is, just because you have the title of "Parent" doesn't mean you are almighty and always right. We are not God. Most of us have to grow into our titles, and we do that by being teachable—even when the lessons come from our children. Ask yourself this question: Am I open to allowing God to teach me through **any** avenue He chooses? Now be real enough with yourself to answer this honestly!

Now you may ask: Aren't we, as adults or parents, supposed to know what is best? Yes, I agree, for the most part. A mature, God-fearing adult should have wisdom, knowledge, and understanding over that of a child. But on those rare occasions where we need our character sharpened, God, if He chooses, can and will use our children. I remember in my undergrad years at Ohio University, Donna, who was one of our Navigators for Christ leaders, shared some thoughts with me. I had just gotten married, and she and I were having a conversation about marriage, home, and family. She said something I really didn't grasp fully, probably because I had no children at the time: "God will fine-tune your character through your children." I thought, oh, okay, that's cool, but I had no idea of the depth of wisdom in her words. So let me pass this on to you, but with a slight revision:

God will fine-tune your character through your children... if you allow Him to.

We can choose to be open, or we can choose to be prideful and turn a deaf ear to anything that exposes flaws in our character. In the earlier example that I shared, I realized that I wasn't angry because my daughter exposed an inconsistency of mine; I was angry because it was exposed, period! I didn't want to change my behavior. I wanted to act out of control at home but paint a different picture when I was in public. Your children see the real you! That's why Donna said, "God will fine-tune your character through your children." It's easy to fake it while you're in public. We dress the part of patient, sweet, loving parent, but when we get home, the out-of-control, undisciplined, hypocritical person comes out. Some of you know that firsthand from living in a home where those at church saw your parents one way, but you had a totally different experience. While there are several reasons why that were the case, the main reason is **PRIDE**. Pride keeps us in a state of self-exhortation.

Let's dive deeper into that word *pride*. It started in the beginning, with Adam and Eve. In Genesis 3:1-6, I found Eve's conversation with the serpent to be particularly interesting. After the serpent questioned God's command, Eve's response to the serpent was that they could eat of every tree in the garden except for the one in the middle, then added a critical statement: GOD says they must not touch it, or they will DIE! Think about that for a minute. If God, the Creator of the universe, says you would die if you touched it, what in the world could the serpent have said that would be so enticing for her to take a chance? PRIDE. The serpent said, "If you eat from it, your eyes will be opened" …and here it is: "You will be like God!" The Bible has many verses about the destructive qualities of pride. It breeds quarrels and conflict (Proverbs 13:10), it precedes destruction (Proverbs 16:18), it brings disgrace and humiliation (Proverbs 11:2, 29:23), just to name a few. Pride will destroy you and your family without you realizing what hit you because it is a position or attitude of your heart. When a person is prideful, it flows through every part of that person, influencing thoughts, words, and actions. It is an attitude of self-righteousness: *I'm right, I know it all, I'm in control, this is what I want.* It's all about "I." What's in the center of the word PRIDE? "I."

Pride is evident through the need to control. For example, with those who expose or resist our pridefulness, we feel the need to beat them down into submission. We continue this abuse until they recognize that we're right. This "beat down" can be through our words as well as our actions.

James 4:6 says that "God opposes the proud but shows favor to the humble." If you want God's favor, then let go of pride. Cry out:

"Lord, I need help! And if You choose for that help to come through my child, then Amen, I receive it."

Can you imagine what your children would be like if you were the opposite of prideful, but humble instead? What if you took advantage of every opportunity to build up your children, encourage them, and awaken the excellence within them? What would your home look like? I think you would be pleasantly surprised, as I was.

I have a confession to make. I still battle with pride. But not in the healthy sense, as Paul shared regarding the church at Corinth,[5] but in a "look what I've done" haughty kind of way. Every time my children receive an award, another degree, recognition, and so on, the temptation is to think that I am an exceptionally great parent who produced these exceptionally great children. The truth is, that without the wisdom of God through these nuggets that I'm sharing with you now, my children would be messed up! Now for those who were raised under the Old School belief that *the parent is always right* and *do as I say, not as I do*, I understand the struggle. Honestly, I get it! But if what I am teaching and living is rooted in pride, my relationship with my child will surely DIE. The truth of the matter is that I am not always right. What saved me and my children's relationship, was when I humbled myself enough to cry out to God that I needed Him, for I could not do this on my own. But this was not a onetime prayer, oh

---

5 "I have the highest confidence in you, and I take great pride in you. You have greatly encouraged me and made me happy despite all our troubles" (2 Corinthians 7:4 NLT).

no. It became a daily surrendering of my pride and submitting to His will.

When I began *Checking My Pride at the Door*, examining myself and getting serious about training the trainer, some wonderful results happened:

> **Better Mom:** I established a Personal Life verse for raising my children (Phil. 4:9[6]) that I strive to live by. I quickly saw results in my life as well as in theirs.

> **Better Communication:** It set a standard. My children believe: *Mom values my opinions and I value hers.* I even bounced ideas off my children to reinforce that I value their opinion. I began by saying, "_____, you have really good ideas about things like this, so what's your opinion about….?" However, let me clarify: I never brought major problems to my children that would cause them to worry. It's not their responsibility to carry the weight of the family.

> **Better Child:** It helped me to learn my children's thinking processes so I could be a better trainer for them. This is important because I, as the parent, needed to understand my child's thinking process. This helped me to guide them in developing sound reasoning skills and conviction, which are critical (we will discuss this topic more in a later chapter). My children became

---

6 Philippians 4:9 KJV: "Those things, which ye have both learned, and received, and heard, and seen in me, do: and the God of peace shall be with you."

"*Overcomers*" when faced with areas of weakness instead of people who passively go along with the crowd.

A word to parents of young children: You may not appreciate good communication with your child when they are three years old, but wait until they are teenagers. You will save yourself much pain and strife if you develop good communication while your children are young. So, here's the next point I want you to:

Put Into Practice

Begin communicating! Resist the urge to criticize, fuss, lecture, or monopolize the conversation during this time. If you're talking longer than 60 seconds at a time, you're monopolizing the conversation! Simply spend time together, just the two of you. This may be more challenging if you have multiple children like me, but it does not have to be a big to-do. I started having tea with my oldest daughter when she was two years old. When my baby girl was born, I included her in our tea parties. They are thirty-eight and forty-one now, and we still have some of our best conversations over tea. For my son, who was less talkative, I bought a Nerf football and we started throwing it to each other. After about five minutes, he started opening up!

Chapter 3

I Can't Hear You...
Because Your Voice Is Too Loud!

My children had a play date, and as the moms were chatting, I noticed one of my children misbehaving, so I excused myself and went to speak with my child. When I returned to the other moms, I received a comment from a very concerned (and stressed-out) parent whose comment was, "You can communicate with your children calmly because they listen. My kids won't listen unless I yell and scream at them!"

First, let me say, I am not confessing that I have never lost my temper, or that my children have ALWAYS listened and obeyed without griping, because that is not the case. I'll admit that I have tried the yelling and screaming tactic, but it did not work. I saw no improvement; as a matter of fact, it made the situation worse. After much prayer, I learned the valuable lesson I shared with you in Chapter 1: I had to Train the Trainer.

I'm going to keep it real.... Who trained your child to only respond to yelling? Are they physically not able to hear you unless you yell? Well, then...stop the yelling! You are proof that "training" works because you trained them to respond to your yelling. That's why you've confessed they listen to others, but not to you. Hopefully, you were able to "Put Into Practice" the suggestions from the previous pages because these are vitally important lessons to learn in awakening the excellence in your child.

I had to learn
to communicate with my children,
not just discipline them.

I had to train
them to Honor their Father and Mother by

teaching them what honor meant.

I had to establish
a foundation of mutual respect;
it doesn't matter if you're young or old, yelling is

insulting and provokes wrath.

It goes back to Training the Trainer (the parent). When I learned to communicate with honor and respect, my children followed suit. So, here's the lesson:

I had to teach
my children to respond to "instruction,"

***not** "emotion."*

I used to feel justified in yelling at my children until I learned this valuable lesson. I recall one day, I was very much out of control, yelling and screaming at my daughter for doing something. About ten minutes after I finally calmed down—I remember just like it was yesterday—her sitting on the steps just bawling her little eyes out. I, being the sensitive parent that I was, yelled, "Child, quit all that crying! What's wrong with you?" And her response was, "You said you don't like me!" My initial response was to deny it, but then I recalled my words. When I was yelling, I said, "**I don't like you** *leaving your toys in the middle of the floor...**I don't like you** doing blah, blah, blah."* To her, my "instructions" were covered up by my lack of self-control, so all she gathered was "I don't like you!" Even though what I said was true and good sound instruction, the lesson was so heavily masked by my emotional tantrum that it was lost! Now what can you deduce from this?

**If my instructions are drowned out by my emotional outbursts…
then the lesson is not learned.
therefore, the child's
behavior will not change.**

If the behavior does not change, then I continue to get angry and start yelling. BUT, if my instructions are drowned out by my emotional outbursts, then the lesson is not learned.....and the cycle continues.

Yelling keeps you and your child in a vicious defeated cycle.

Don't get caught up in this emotional cycle, or you will become a yelling out-of-control monster, and you will train your children to become one, too. Now please, please, please…don't even try to justify your lack of self-control by saying that Jesus got angry and threw the folk out the temple[7] because the context was different. Jesus was dealing with money-hungry, irreverent ADULTS, not children. Controlled anger has its proper place in raising children. There is much we experience in life that should make us angry to the point of despising them,[8] but do not get confused. This type of anger is different from yelling and lacking self-control. Furthermore, when a child is trained to respond only to emotion, the repercussions trickle into their student life, relationships, and parenthood. So here are two challenges I offer to you:

7 Matthew 21:12, Holy Bible (KJV)

8 Proverbs 6:16-19, Holy Bible (KJV).

PUT INTO PRACTICE

1. Stop making excuses for your lack of self-control. Your high stress level, your own insecurity, and even your child's disobedience do not justify your yelling and insulting them.

2. When tempted to "lose control," simply confess (I used to say this out loud to my children), "I will not raise my voice. You are an obedient child who listens to instruction." Sometimes, I would have to get up close and in their face to get their attention. Then, I would continue and state clearly—and calmly—what I expected of them. Keep it simple! If you're talking with younger children for more than 15 seconds, chances are, you've lost their attention and unfortunately, the behavior will not change. So be concise and calm. Remember, this is a training process that may not change overnight, but if you are dillgent, your training will pay off.

Principle #3:

Understand the power of your words

Chapter 4

Two Negatives Don't Equal a Positive

First things first. I want each of you to know that I pray for every reader who reads this book because teaching your child to respond to instruction instead of emotion can be an enormous task. Please do not be weary in well doing as this chapter should help you and your child gain success more quickly.

Remember math class when you were a student? You learned if you multiply two negatives, it will produce a positive. Well, that rule does **not** apply to raising our children.

Negative actions of a child, when **multiplied by Negative** comments from the parent
do not result in a Positive outcome.

Saying this now sounds a little silly, but when my children were performing negatively, I would begin complaining, telling them all the negative things I saw in their behavior. For some reason, I actually believed that would generate a positive result! I was only fooling myself. I later learned by applying the following that children respond more positively:

> First, make sure your children know **you** *EXPECT* positive behavior. Once again, this may sound a bit silly, but how many times has your child messed up and the first remark out of your mouth was "I knew you were going to blow it!" You expected them to mess up and, more importantly, **they knew** you expected them to mess up.

> Second (and this is very important to awakening the excellence in your child), they must know that **you SEE** the potential in them to overcome the negative behavior. Even the most disobedient child wants their parent to be proud of them.

Although not intentionally, I put this into practice before I had children when I interacted with my niece. I would tell her what an obedient and kind child she was. This was and still is the truth. As a result, whenever she was around me, she lived up to **my expectations**. But I never **learned the lesson** until years later when I had my children. Let me explain.

I love the fact that my children are very "no nonsense," especially my baby girl. She is very direct and does not mince words. In her younger years, she lacked finesse. To be blunt, she was very offensive. As a result, when she was in elementary school, she had the reputation of being "mean" to those who were offended by her straightforward manner. I felt I was in a losing battle as I attempted to discipline her for the bad behavior while at the same time teaching her that her words should be *seasoned with grace.* So, I once again cried out to God for wisdom. The lesson God taught me was to replace my old comments of "That was mean to say…stop being so mean and…why are you so mean…mean, mean, mean!" with words affirming her potential. Now don't get me wrong: I strongly believe wrong behavior should be punished, and it was, but not verbally (refer to Chapter 3). I had to train myself to speak those qualities I desired her to become.

Stop speaking what they are and start speaking what they will become.

As parents, we have the awesome privilege through our words to either keep our children where they are or remind them of what they can become. Some of us today are still battling with the negative words our parents spoke over us twenty or thirty-plus years ago. But, instead of changing, we speak the same detrimental thoughts to our children. It is time to stop. You know it is wrong, and you can and will do better! You must train your mind to think and your mouth to confess what you desire to become.

I noted in an earlier chapter that I would re-visit the topic of the "middle child" and why I will never refer to my baby girl that way. Whenever the term "middle child" is used, it is most often in a sentence describing the problems that surround growing up as a middle child.

I love this quote by Dr. William James, the famous Harvard psychology professor and author, who said: "Human beings, by changing the inner attitudes of their minds, can change the outer aspects of their lives." Knowing the truth of this lesson, I had to make a choice. I could either join in with others who labeled my daughter as being "mean," or I could speak what I desired her to become. I chose the latter. I made it a point to tell her everyday what a sweet girl she was. Whenever she said or did something not in line with the sweet girl she was becoming, I would return to the two bullet points I listed above: make sure she understood the behavior I expected and knew that I saw in her the potential to be kind and gracious. I would periodically remind her she was a sweet girl throughout the day and always at night before she went to bed. This did not happen overnight, but as the weeks went on, I could see her behavior change. She also embraced this lesson and even now at the age of thirty-eight when I tell her I love her and remind her she is a sweet girl, she responds, "You're a sweet girl too, Mommy."

Put Into Practice

1. Say something positive to your child three times a day. Don't turn it into a lecture; keep it simple and genuine. For example, "You're a good listener," "You're a kind big brother," or "You're my best helper." Later, you will find an area you may want to key in on and strengthen. When you do, I suggest encouraging them when you put your children to bed so they can meditate on what you're speaking over them.

2. Remember two negatives do not make a positive, so even when you discipline them, speak what you want them to become. For example, "No, son, you cannot watch TV because you did not clean up your room. You are very good at organizing things, so when I come back in fifteen minutes, I know you will have made great progress, and then we can discuss watching TV." Be consistent and steadfast.... Rome wasn't built in a day!

Chapter 5

Use Your Words...Wisely

Children are influenced by both teaching and leading. Teaching is depositing or delivering information, and leading is a practical application of the information that is taught. So, both play a critical role in awakening excellence in your child.

In the previous chapters, we discussed training the trainer or leading by example. In this chapter, I want to key in on our words—how we are delivering information to our children through how we use our words.

Words are very powerful. They can bring about healing or death, promote restoration or cause division, build up or tear down. They can live in us for a moment, or they can live for a lifetime. The Bible has much to say about what we speak. In Proverbs alone, we see many examples. Proverbs 15:4 says gentle words bring life and health; a deceitful tongue crushes the spirit. Proverbs 16:24 says kind words are like honey, sweet to the soul and healthy for the body. Proverbs 18:4 says a person's words can be life-giving water; words of true wisdom are as refreshing as a bubbling brook. These are all examples of how the right words even cause our bodies to be healthy. So, why is it so difficult for us to master what we say?

I often think back on the book of Genesis about how God formed the world. He formed the world with the words from His mouth. He spoke and all came into being (Rom. 4:17, Heb. 11:13). When He formed us, He formed us in His image, meaning He formed us after the likeness of Himself. When he breathed life into us, this life came with authority! Now we do not have the ability to create something out of nothing; only God our Creator can do that. But unlike any of His other creations, we human beings have the authority to speak words, such as the verses I shared earlier from Proverbs. Thus, these words and our words bring life, health, joy, and many other benefits.

Words can bring about so much healing, but they can also do much damage in awakening the excellence in your child, so I must address the subject and address it strongly! I believe we all can agree that yelling and name calling are wrong. So, why do we do it? It is a fleshly desire that is quickly accessible. Think about it: To gossip, slander, or retaliate takes no extra effort or preparation. All we need is one small tool...our tongues. James 3:1-11 put it so simply by describing how such a small member of our body can be used to create so much damage. But the tongue is just the instrument used. In truth, the heart is where everything originates. I love the way that the Contemporary English Bible states it: "Good people do good things because of the good in their hearts. Bad people do bad things because of the evil in their hearts. Your words show what is in your heart" (Luke 6:45).

To correct a bad behavior, we must first *want to make* a *change*; it is not enough only to recognize that a change is needed. We must desire it so much that we will do whatever it takes to accomplish it. This starts with a change of heart! I wish we could see, literally, the power that words have over our children. Not just their present state, but also their futures.

When I saw how my edifying words spoken over my daughter, even though others were talking negatively about her, began to change her behavior, my desire to change my own behavior grew even more. My strong desire brought about a conscious and intentional action. Let's look at *action* with a different example, which most of us can relate to.

Perhaps you want to lose weight. You may desire to see a change in your weight, but if you're not committed enough to get up off that couch and stop eating cookies, cakes, ice cream, and all that bad food, it will not matter how much you desire. You simply will not lose weight! But what if you wanted to lose weight so that you could look good for your 25th high school reunion? Everything would change. Your actions surrounding what you did and what you ate would change because you really, really desire to lose weight to look your best.

Now, let's bring this example to how desire is demonstrated in communicating with your child. If you really desire to see a change in your behavior, especially in the way you talk to your children, first, know that you can do it! Your reading this book is a demonstration that your heart is in the right place to be better. To change bad behavior, we must replace it with good behavior. Set in place clear steps that will consciously produce a change in behavior. These changes do not come forth from your desire only. There are other external and internal changes you may need to make to begin moving in the right direction.

Let's look again at the earlier example I used about losing weight. You will need to change many aspects of your life. For example, you may need to disconnect from people who constantly overeat. You may need to change your grocery shopping habits to avoid the aisles with junk food and other products that will divert you from the right direction. You may need to read articles on how to remove sugary items from your diet and replace them with healthier choices. I admit it is not easy to change undesirable behavior. But it is possible. We will discuss some practical steps in the "Put Into Practice" section, but for now, I want you to think about people, things, and old habits that promote poor communication.

How can you make some changes? What needs to be cut out? Also, think about what should be added. Matthew Henry states in his commentary of James 3: "No man can tame the tongue without supernatural grace and assistance." Amen, Brother Henry! We must be willing to submit our fleshy nature to God and **walk** in the Spirit. One area that helped me tremendously was scripture memory. I would write a Bible verse on a card and post it on the refrigerator. The verse would be uplifting and encouraging. It reminded me I am in charge of my speech, and I should use it to build up, not tear down my children. This action actually had a twofold benefit: it not only helped me but, as a result, my children would see the verse and ask why it was on the refrigerator. I had a chance to tell them these verses were reminding me of how precious my children are, and that I have a responsibility to God about how I use my words with them. Now I must admit that change did not happen overnight. I still had many days where I said words that did not build up my children. However, I did see a change eventually. I would always tell the following to my children whenever they endeavor to make a character change:

Change, even when it's for the best, is not easily received.

That holds true for the person making the change as well as for those who will receive the benefits of the change. I know you're saying, "If I stop yelling and insulting my child, are you claiming they may not welcome it?" That is exactly what I am saying. Let me explain. If you have, for years, communicated to your child through yelling and insults, but then begin talking in a peaceful, controlled tone, they may not, *in the beginning,* respond to what you're saying. That is why discipline is key—for you and your child. You have to train yourself first to speak *like you've got good* sense, and they will learn, in time, to respond in the same manner.

James 3:10 states that with our same mouth, we bless God and curse people (our children). Yes, when you scold your children and utter such statements as "You're just like your good-for-nothing daddy" or "I told you to pick that up, you don't listen," you are, with your words, slandering your child. When you read this, I admit it sounds harsh, ugly, and even scary. But truly, it is all that. I heard a mother tell her son, who was crying because of his father's angry insults, that "It's okay. He didn't mean it. He was just angry." I thought, wow, is that supposed to make her son feel better? Is her son supposed to stop crying and respond, "Oh, well, since I know he was angry, I feel so much better about being called all those mean things." That's preposterous! Our anger does not give us the right to curse another human being who is made in the image of God. But we have been programmed to feel that we should be excused from being held accountable for defaming others simply because we were angry. What a contradiction!

That is why it is vitally important not to discipline when you're angry…take ten seconds, thirty seconds, even a full minute if you need to. But don't wait too long because children also forget quickly what they've done wrong. It is a matter of you exercising discipline before you discipline your child. How can you get your child in control if you are out of control? When we speak in anger, our words become confusing, and our children, especially when very young, cannot **decipher** what we say from what we mean. Here is an example that I referred to earlier. When my daughter was very young, I remember disciplining her and she began to cry hysterically because she heard me say that I did not like her. The truth was that I loved her, but I did not like her actions at that particular time. This is what I mean by *decipher*. We must help our children properly interpret, work through, or make sense of what we are teaching them.

In the above example, my words produced an action in my daughter: tears, rejection, hurt. However, if that had been left unresolved, it could have planted the seed of *Mommy doesn't like me*. That seed could grow into an attitude of *Mommy likes my sister or brother more than me*. Eventually, the seed could blossom into jealousy between siblings. This may seem extreme, but some of us are walking around today with envy or hatred for our family members, planted in us by our parents, and we don't even know when it began.

PUT INTO PRACTICE

1. If you have made it a practice of harming your child through your speech, stop now, pray, and ask God for forgiveness and strength. Ask God to help you to forgive those who have harmed you with their words.

2. Gradually, remove some of the stresses or triggers from your life and replace them with healthier habits. This may involve people, places, or bad habits you will need to let go of. Incorporate scriptures, songs, and people that align with your new desired behavior.

Chapter 6

"Put-Me-Downs"

In the Bible, we read of all the great and mighty wonders of God that happened when we little ol' human beings call upon a mighty God in faith. Jeremiah 33:3 states: "Call upon me and I will answer thee and show thee great and mighty things which thou knowest not." So, if God's Word is true, which it is, then this verse suggests that when we, as believers, call upon our God, He is committed to answering us. Not only answering us, but also responding in such a way that we will have to stop and say, "WOW!... I never would have thought that would happen to me in a million years!"

Isn't it interesting that God CHOOSES to bless us through our request of Him? It parallels how we tell our children after they ask for something. We say, "How do you ask?" and we wait for them to say "please." It is not that we don't know what they're asking for, nor is it that we have no means or intentions of giving it to them. But it is the STANDARD that we have set for receiving what they desire. This is not to suggest that the *only* time God moves is when we ask Him to do so because the sun rises and the moon sets without our asking. However, it does suggest that God, for whatever reason, has declared He is moved to action by our words or communication to Him. "Call upon Me, ask and it shall be given, let your requests be made known, you have not because you ask not...." God is omniscient, yet numerous times in the Bible, He requires us to ask. "Why?" It's His **STANDARD**.

This led me to think what standards have I set up in my house that govern our relationships with each other? What governs our normal, everyday behavior?

One of the standards that God laid upon my heart after the birth of my second child concerned our words. We are NEVER allowed to use "put-me-downs." That means we cannot speak badly about ourselves or each other. It does not matter if we are angry, confused, sad, or joking. Put-me-downs are not acceptable anytime nor anywhere.

This was going to be a challenge for me, because put-me-downs were often used when I was growing up, sometimes by adults, but mainly by children. It was common to use put-me-downs jokingly or confrontationally. We would call someone stupid or ugly or make fun of them because they were "different." I know that was mean, but that is what we did.

There is an old saying I first heard in elementary school from a teacher:

Sticks and stones may break my bones,
but names will never hurt me.

I think my teacher taught it to us so that she would not have to mediate every name-calling argument—

which, in my elementary school, was very frequent.

This phrase may sound cute, but we all know it was not the truth. As I grew up, what I experienced was quite the opposite: sticks and stones will hurt my bones, but physical hurt, most of the time, will heal. However, verbal abuse—whether sporadic name-calling or repetitive degrading insults—can live forever.

Sometimes when we get angry, we'll "blow up" and then once we've calmed down, we think it's all over. We fail to realize all the damage we have done. Many of you reading this right now were probably told negative things about yourself over and over when you were a child, and even now as an adult, you still wrestle with those memories. Some words may have been said jokingly, but nevertheless were put-me-downs that hurt you, and you are still haunted by them today.

Now you may be thinking: Oh, I don't call my children names, nor do I allow put-me-downs to be shared among my children. But I want you to think about another form of put-me-downs that you may not have thought about in the past. This is disguised as a "prayer request" or "venting" or simply "getting someone's opinion." Discussing my child's shortcomings to someone else could be viewed as a betrayal of trust. This can be very damaging not only to your child but also to your family unit. We as parents play a vital role in developing this attribute of trust in our children. Unfortunately, the first lessons on how **not** to trust come through the betrayal of trust exhibited by our family interactions.

I will ask you once again to go back down memory lane and remember a time when you found out that your parent or guardian was saying something negative about you to someone else, or worse, to another family member, like a sibling. How did that make you feel? And honestly, is that what we want our children to feel? No. Then why do we do it?

This goes back to what I said at the beginning of this chapter…we lack the desire and discipline to change. We are not willing to submit our fleshy nature to God and walk in the Spirit. I know we make excuses and say we are upset and *need* to vent. Or we disguise it as a prayer request, so we will feel better about sharing personal information about others. We start out by saying, "Girl, pray for me because this child is getting on my last nerve," then proceed to share every detail that happened. Most of the time, when we finish sharing our "prayer request", praying is the furthest thought from your mind! God spoke to me one time when I was about to open my mouth and complain about my child to someone. He made me aware that

**If I am *truly committed*
to seeing this behavior changed in my child,
then I must talk to Him about it
twice as much as I talk to anyone else….
including my child.**

This really stopped me dead in my tracks. First, I had to humble myself and ask, "Do I really want to see the behavior changed, or do I just want to complain about it?" Sometimes we even continue to complain about our child's misbehavior, even after the unacceptable behavior has been corrected. If I corrected the behavior, then I need to let it go. Quit nagging and complaining about it; and, by all means, quit raising it again months or even years later. No one wants to hear all that except you.

What helped me most was to understand how talking negatively about my child could be considered a put-me-down. All I had to do was, just for a moment, look at my children as though they were adults. How would I feel if I walked into a room and saw two people talking about me—one being my best friend? It would not matter why my best friend felt the need to share my personal business, but what would matter was simply that my best friend shared it. I would feel a flood of emotions; anger, hurt, and disappointed. I would also feel my trust had been betrayed.

Did you know that a study on human emotions, conducted at UC Berkeley, found that humans can experience twenty-seven different emotions?[9] But most of us live in the ballpark of identifying only seven or eight—less than one-third of our emotions.

For children, it may be less than that. Thus, when they hear us talking negatively about them to someone else, the feelings and emotions they feel are the same as when someone calls them a name or makes fun of them.

Don't get me wrong. There are times we legitimately need to "share our burdens one with another" and receive counseling. Sometimes you need

9 Yasmin Anwar, "How Many Different Human Emotions Are There?" September 8, 2017. https://greatergood.berkeley.edu/

to have someone else pray for you and with you about whatever your child is going through. The effective fervent prayer of the righteous availeth much![10] So, I believe getting sound counsel from others is beneficial and biblical. The book of Proverbs is full of instructions on the benefits of wise counsel.

When that is the case, just make certain that you check your heart and your motives. Ask yourself these questions: Do you just want to vent, complain, or gossip? Have you taken this concern earnestly to God first? Is the person you're sharing this with considered to be wise counsel? If my child was within earshot of my conversation, would they feel put down or betrayed? If you honestly feel that your child would feel disrespected or betrayed by you sharing information, then you can certainly give your prayer request without names and specific details. And you certainly do not need to go on and on and on about the problem. Remember, God is the One that moves in the hearts of our children to change their attitudes and actions, NOT US.

To this day, I make it a practice never to talk negatively about one of my children to their siblings (and my youngest is in his mid-thirties). This is a difficult practice because when we all lived together, it was hard to be disciplined when the opportunity arises to vent so soon after the offense was made. But I have seen firsthand the damage that talking negatively does to the family unit. On the flip side, my children know this is a standard we have set in our home, so it adds to their sense of security and builds their level of trust.

10 "The effectual fervent prayer of the righteous availeth much." James 5:16 King James Version.

PUT INTO PRACTICE

Stop talking negatively about your children to others, especially other family members. Put-me-downs only breed insecurities. Instead, intentionally brag on your child to others where they can hear you speaking words of praise about them. Soon, they will begin to live up to the level of your edifying words!

Principle #4:
Focus on Character not Rules

Chapter 7

Rule #1· Quit Having So Many Rules!

I was raised Old School, and my father made it very clear that if I was going to live in his house, then I was going to follow his rules! So, when I had my children, that became my motto too…until one of my children ran away from home. Yes, you read that right! When that happened, I had to stop and re-evaluate everything very seriously.

You may think there is nothing wrong with such a motto; after all, don't children need to have set boundaries? Absolutely! But usually this statement, and others like it, is disguised as an emotional threat, which most definitely will *not* awaken the excellence in your child (refer to the last chapter). So, let's examine this statement more closely.

If you're going to live in my house, you're going to follow my rules.

"IF" implies there's a choice…. Well, when I made this statement to my children, I was not prepared to live with the consequences of them choosing to leave, and neither were they. Even though my heart was saying, "I want you to live peaceably in this house with me," my mouth and actions were giving them an ultimatum.

When we make statements like this, it's really a cry for help because we feel tired and helpless. It's exhausting butting heads with your child; after all, you're sacrificing money, sleep, personal enjoyment… and they have the nerve to act disrespectfully, disobediently, and ungratefully! Most of all, you feel helpless because nothing you've tried works. Right now, you're probably saying, "*WHATEVER, lady! The bottom line is that they are the child and I am the adult, and if they're going to live in my house, then they're going to follow my rules!*"

Ok, I hear you, but let's be real. Is this (or any of your other threats) working? Did it work when you were a child and your parents threatened you with statements like these? Most of us thought, "I can't wait until I'm eighteen, so I won't have to deal with you or your rules!"

Your children may or may not move out of your home at eighteen, but they certainly will not master an attitude of obedience because of your threats. But isn't that the goal for saying this? Your desire behind saying such a statement is that you want your child to be obedient. You want your children to live peaceably at home until they are old enough and responsible enough to make it successfully on their own. But giving ultimatums will not lead to obedience! So, why do we continue to say such statements again and again and again, thinking they will produce the right attitude of obedience and submission? Threats only lead to rebellion, which leads to more blowups, which leads back to more threats, which leads to more blowups… and the cycle continues. It's like watching a re-run of the same movie many times, but somehow expecting the end result to be different.

Well, let me share another saying with you: "If you always do what you've always done, then you'll always get what you've always gotten!"

Threats do not awaken excellence. Rather, they are emotional outbursts that produce temporary changes. Some of us have so many rules that we can't even keep up with them. We put unexpected pressures on ourselves and our children to live up to a standard designed for failure. Then, when our child breaks a rule, we're right there to add two or three more rules onto our list.

This reminds me of a passage in the Bible in Genesis 26:5. It states, " Abraham obeyed my voice and kept my charge, my commandments, my statutes, and laws." The first set of rules were given directly from God to Moses. The Bible does not state how many rules, but the Bible does state, Moses obey the voice and kept His commandments. But then something happened. After Moses led the children of Israel out of Egypt, on Mount Sinai, God gave the children of Israel the Ten Commandments (Exo. 20:1-17). As time went on, the Ten Commandments grew to 613, covering every aspect of life: personal hygiene, family, diet, law, among many others.[11]

The rules did not make them a submissive and grateful people. The rules did not give them a heart of obedience, and the rules certainly did not bring them any closer to God.

So, what's the difference between Abraham and the Children of Egypt? Why did Abraham, when given a list of rules, obey, but the children of Israel did the opposite? The answer is this; Abraham believed God, and this belief overflowed into a heart of righteous obedience. Abraham DESIRED to please God because he had a relationship with God (Gen. 15:6; Romans 4:3).

Initially, I made my children like the Israelites, trying to keep all the laws of the Old Testament, because I was under the false assumption that my many rules would lead my children into living a successful life. So, I began to study the scriptures. The purpose of the Laws was to be our trainer, schoolmaster, guardian, leading us to faith in the promise of Christ. With that in mind, my aim in awakening the excellence in my children changed from having them follow my long list of rules to pointing them to a relationship with Christ. Through that relationship, they developed their faith, conviction, and good character. This became one of my principles for raising children of excellence:

Work on building godly character
instead of a list of rules.

11 https://www.bbc.co.uk/judaism/history/moses

Here's why building a godly character is so important. Whether your child is 6 or 16, eventually they are going to be out of your sight, and you will not be able to threaten them into obedience. There may come a time when you are not the loudest voice in their head. *They will have to choose* whether to do right or wrong, and no matter how strict and mighty you may think you are, your "rules" are not going to stop them from making a wrong choice.

Think of it this way: What if you told your child not to touch the stove? But what if you didn't teach them that when the stove is on, it is hot and it will harm you, burn you, and leave a scar? If you didn't teach them that part, guess what will happen when you turn your back? They're going to touch the stove! This will happen because they haven't built conviction, they don't know the WHY, they don't have a foundation of what's good and what's bad, what's right and what's wrong.

So, build conviction.

That is why we as parents must focus on character more than behavior. But let's face it: we want to see quick results, so most parents focus on behavior when they want their kids to be obedient. They have many rules for them to follow, and if they don't follow them, then they are punished. But, then what happens when the child gets older, moves away, and must make their own rules to live by? They run the risk of failing because they do not know how to make good, sound decisions.

You have to build a sound foundation…you have to build conviction. You have to teach them and talk with them and explain WHY it is that God desires them to follow this path.

Think of this as expanding the way you taught them when they were very young. Remember the earlier example; never to touch the stove? As our kids grow older, they need to understand the principles behind the guidelines and boundaries we have set up for them, not just the consequences of disobedience. They need to know why we live the way we live and what is behind the guidelines we have set for them.

God doesn't have a bunch of rules, but He has a plan for them that involves a prosperous and abundant life.

I prayed and asked God to teach me how to build a Godly conscience, and here is the lesson He taught me. The first step was for me to learn to pick my battles. I did not have to jump in and control every situation, especially when it came to settling daily sibling quarrels. I had to learn to let some things go for the present and learn to say, "You both make good decisions, so you work it out." I learned that some battles I did not need to fight verbally every day because it caused me to be viewed as the *Attacker* instead of the *Builder*. Let me explain. An attacker destroys, but a builder creates and restores. An attacker invades, but a builder can be trusted. Then God reminded me of this, as I mentioned before:

If I am *truly committed* to seeing behavior changed in my child, then I must talk to Him about it *twice* as much as I talk to anyone else....including my child.

The greatest obstacle I faced with this challenge was getting over the need to hear myself talk. As quiet as it's kept, some of you, will need to get over this too. When my children were younger, I fussed, lectured, whined, and complained, but nothing seemed to get through. However, when I was committed to praying more and talking less, I saw results. The older my children got, the fewer rules I needed to have. Rules are made for the unruly. As I built godliness, the unruliness decreased, and so the need for rules lessened. Every parent wants their children to be successful in life, so focus on building their character, not on them keeping all of your rules. When you do that, in the words of three-time Super Bowl winner Bill Walsh, "The score takes care of itself."

PUT INTO PRACTICE

1. Simply pray. Every day this week, pray for yourself and your children.

2. Pray that your mouth speaks the love you have in your heart for them.

3. Pray that you stop threatening but instead start confessing what you desire your relationship to become with your children.

4. Pray that you learn the importance of talking less and listening more.

Chapter 8

Training Through the Power of a Question

When growing up, we could not conversationally question an adult. It was a sign of disrespect. A child asking a question to an adult was viewed as questioning their authority. My parents wanted to teach me the importance of being obedient. Their instructions were to be followed to the "t"—no questions asked. It was also a matter of trust. Don't worry about why they told you to do something; instead, you were simply to trust that whatever you were told—it was the best for you. The bottom line was that my parents were not going to stop and explain every command given. They felt if they had to give an explanation **before** I was obedient, it could cost me my life in extreme instances. Can you imagine if I was playing on the sidewalk and my mother saw a car coming down the street and it was swerving, and she said, "Patty, get on this porch right now!" and I hesitated to ask why. Well, I'll just say, I wouldn't be writing this right now for a number of reasons!

While I understand and agree somewhat with the premise behind not asking questions however, I don't believe it laid a solid foundation for building conviction.

Now please hear me out. I understand if you may have a raised eyebrow at what I just stated because, honestly, I wrestled with this as well. Remember, I was raised Old School.

There is a time for healthy, respectful Q&A, but if this openness is not initiated by the parent, the child will not feel the comfort and assurance needed to engage. Yet don't worry, your child is not going to be confused about when is an appropriate time to ask why. As they mature, most children learn their parents' voice tone, body language, and energy surrounding dangerous situations, so having an immediate response of obedience becomes somewhat of a reflex. As you engage in natural conversation, they will begin to understand the meaning behind what they should and should not do.

For a moment, think about the benefits of your child feeling comfortable to ask you any question about any subject, personal or not. Wouldn't that be great if your child came to you first, before going to a friend or someone they just met to ask questions about dating, money management, relationships, careers, and so on? The ease of being able to talk to a parent comes from having open and honest conversations about day-to-day things. It becomes a part of their everyday life. Say, for example, your child comes home from school and says, "Emily asked me if I wanted one of her cigarettes after school when we were walking home, and I didn't know how to respond." If your child is comfortable bringing that to you, well, then you can help her talk through why that is or is not a good choice and how she could respond to her friend by going through various scenarios. Do you see the steps to asking questions, and how you as the parent lead, not dictate, them into conversation, which allows them to build conviction?

Then, once they can openly talk through the question, then you can assist in helping them understand it. That way, THEY will learn how to desire the best for THEMSELVES and will want to stay away from anything that will harm them.

Wouldn't it be great if each child came with an owner's manual, where if you followed Steps 1 through 18, the end result would be a well-adjusted, successful adult who loved God and fellow man? While that would be wonderful, we know that children don't come with a manual. I believe the Bible is "a lamp to our feet and a light to our path," but it does not contain step-by-step instructions for just your child. You have to be led by the Spirit and operate with discernment because each of us is an individual with many facets. Your child has a unique personality, and if taught well, is capable of making good and sound decisions. I think the individuality of your child is part of the excitement—and sometimes part of the fear—of raising children.

So spice it up! When your child gets home from school, instead of asking the usual "How was your day? or "Do you have any homework?" change that up and maybe ask, "What did you learn in English today?"

or "I know you were working on a big assignment in science. What was it about?" But here's the most important bit: After they've answered your question, quick—give them a word of encouragement. It may be in the form of a compliment, or some extraordinary thing you noticed they did that week. But be sincere! Just as children have to learn to engage, so do we as parents. Questions that are open-ended are engaging and tend to be less judgmental. For example, the conversation at the dinner table could go like this:

> *Scenario #1*
>
> *Mom: "Did you have a good day?" (closed-ended question that requires a yes or no answer).*
>
> *Child: "Yes."*
>
> *End of conversation*
>
> *Scenario #2*
>
> *Mom: "Today, there was an ant in the kitchen and it made me think about my sixth-grade teacher, Mrs. Huckabuck. She told us that she went on vacation and ate chocolate-covered ants! Yuk! So what's your funniest sixth grade memory?" (engaging, open-ended question)*

In Scenario #2, your child has (a) an opportunity to learn something new about you, and (b) you've communicated that you're interested in learning something new about your child.

Questions open the door for teaching opportunities, and children need to be taught how to make good decisions. Unfortunately, this comes by trial and error. Isn't it weird how we expect our children to never make mistakes? Think about it whenever our child messes up…we get on them for messing up. Now I'm not talking about messing up, as in your child not cleaning their room *again* and this is the *fifth* time you've asked them to do it. I'm talking about new experiences, such as running out of time to finish a school project. What if you looked at that mess-up in a different way? What if that mess-up was an opportunity to teach your child how to go through "the process of making a good decisions" or "time management techniques"?

Now, if we continue with the example that I used to not have enough time to finish a school project, I would wait until after my child has turned in the project to the teacher. But this is the perfect opportunity for you to teach your child about time management. The Old School method would be to get a calendar and post it in their room so they could write down all of the projects that are due during each six weeks; then, from there, YOU could determine how much time it would take to complete the project. While calendars today would be on their phone, of course, there are still no guarantees that your child will not wait until the last minute to work on a project. Nevertheless, it is our job to put in the time to train them.

Remember, in the first chapter of this book on "train the trainer," I referenced the verse in Proverbs 22:6, which states: *Train a child in the way they should go, and when they are old they will not turn from it.*

Training involves understanding the power of asking a question. You see, questions allow you to see how your child deciphers information. What process do they use in making decisions?

Let me share with you a true story. An acquaintance of mine had a beautiful daughter named Sally (the name has been changed to respect her anonymity). She did well in school and was polite, active in her church, and beloved by everyone. Sally's Mom and Dad were devoted Christians and felt the best way to raise her was to make all her decisions. They told Sally what to do and what not to do in **every** circumstance. She lived by an extremely short list of "do's" but an extremely long list of "don'ts." When Sally went away to college, as you probably guessed, she went *buck wild!* While hearing of one bad story after another regarding Sally was difficult, it also left me confused. How could such a sweet girl with so much promise *and* who was raised by Christian parents drop out of college, shack up with a man who abused her, start doing drugs, drinking and smoking, and live a life so opposite to what she knew to be right? As I prayed for Sally and her family as well as for understanding, God impressed upon my heart this thought: Sally had never learned to think on her own. She was good at following orders, but she was never good at assessing a situation and then making the best decision based on her personal convictions. So, whenever someone who was very controlling and dominant came into her life and told her what she needed to do and what she should not do, she fell into the usual pattern that was drilled into her from birth to high school—follow instructions. Now some of you may be thinking why couldn't Sally just make up her own mind when she knew things were not good to do? That was her fault!......

But take off your halos just for a moment and imagine yourself in Sally's shoes. The first time she moved away from her parents' supervision, she was just trying to have a good time. One event led to another. It wasn't a drastic crossover to the dark side, actually, but a step-by-step process of someone saying, "Oh, it's okay. If you really love me…" It was a series of one-time scenarios: When you add them all up, Sally was living a life of going along with the flow. So the question I had to ask myself was: Am I raising children who follow me, or am I developing **children with conviction?**

"Training a child in the way they should go" means to develop within your child convictions rather than rituals.

Rituals are customs…things your child will do when Mom and Dad are present. But convictions are beliefs. In other words, this is what your child believes in and, more importantly, what your child will follow, whether Mom and Dad are present or not. Here is my next question: How do I, as a parent, develop conviction in my children? Through *self-discovery*. Through the power of your questions, **the child** realizes the truth and is confident in **their** decision. Think about it: When *you* go through *your* thought process while making a decision, you consider the "why's," not just the "do's and don'ts." When you learn the "why's," you develop convictions, not just rituals, because questions help us determine our purpose and direction. Our children learn the same way.

Obedience must, I repeat, must come from the heart, or it becomes nothing more than a performance. Once the audience is gone, the act is over.

A choice is made from their beliefs that the choice is what they want because they know what is best for them. I know it's easier to simply tell your child what not to do, and that is wonderful—even appropriate—when they are young. But the goal is not to continue to make decisions for them for the rest of your life. That enabling behavior only builds insecurities and causes resentment when they are older.

When my children began elementary school, I started slowly **teaching them** how to reason and correctly think through options. At the dinner table, I would create various scenarios. Then, I would ask questions like "What do you think about that?" or "Why do you think they responded the way they did?" or "Can you think of a better way they could have handled that?" I was not only getting to know their thought processes, but I was also training them in ways to handle situations and, more importantly, I was helping them to develop conviction. I was teaching them *why* they should respond the way they do instead of simply *how* to respond. By the time they reached high school, there was no need to have a long list of rules to govern their behavior. I never set a curfew, restricted hours of phone usage, or felt the need to nag them to call me every five minutes when they went out because I raised children of conviction! And, remember, I did not have one child nor two children; I had three children with very different personalities. It was simply amazing! Was the journey easy leading up to high school? No! Did I feel like giving up? Yes, many times. But I stood on my conviction that Proverbs 22:6 was true, so I trained and prayed, then prayed some more and kept on training!

This **"Put Into Practice"** is somewhat different. Questions are powerful, but our children must feel engaged in conversation with us. Their comfort level will be determined by how you respond to their questions and comments. Are you judgmental or are you truly listening? Do you wait until they're finished before commenting? I believe the best teaching moments happen naturally in our everyday occurrences; however, sometimes it's good to plan a special exercise to focus on certain topics. Hopefully, you will give the following a try.

PUT INTO PRACTICE

Write on slips of paper the names of a few relevant topics and put them in a bag (for example, drugs, pornography, bullying, premarital sex, stealing, peer pressure, alcohol, lying, etc.). Let your child pick from the bag and then use that topic for a family discussion. It may be difficult to do this during dinnertime, but be creative and do whatever works best for your family. Parents, you should facilitate the discussion and have a list of open-ended questions each week that generate discussion. For example, if the topic is drugs, you may ask:

➤ What are drugs?

➤ What does doing drugs lead to?

➤ Who do we know has battled with drugs? (Have short articles with examples of those who chose to go down that road and discuss their testimonies.)

➤ Does doing drugs only affect the individual? Discuss how drug use eventually destroys the individual and their relationships with family and friends.

➤ Do you feel that doing drugs is something you should engage in?

➤ What does God say about our caring for our bodies?

➢ How can you respond when you're confronted by peers on the topic of drugs? Then go through scenarios so that your child can practice responding with words that are comfortable for them.

As the discussion time progresses, *your questions* should help lead your children in the right direction for developing convictions of their own. Have a Bible, dictionary, or computer available for each session. Avoid the temptation of taking over the conversation and making it a lecture. If you're talking more than sixty seconds at a time…you're talking too much!

Principle #5:
Pray more, talk less

Chapter 9

Pray Without Ceasing· The Prayer

Today, as I sat down to write, I thought, I really don't **feel** like doing much of anything. Have you ever experienced days like this? There were many days when my children were young when I could have stayed in the bed with a pizza…oh, and some butter pecan ice cream…until my children were grown! Parenting isn't always convenient; we cannot say to our child "I'm staying in bed this week" when they need a ride to soccer practice, help with homework, encouragement over a bad day, or counsel for their decision making. We may be able to squeeze in a couple of hours for ourselves without interruption, but for the most part, parenting is a 24/7 adventure. I'll admit I was not Super Woman; even though I had great desire, I had limited knowledge, patience, and energy. Am I by myself here?

Regardless of how I'm feeling at the present, I know what an awesome honor it is to raise children. Do you realize everything else on this earth in which you invest your time will pass away, but what you invest in your child will determine their eternity? So,

79

let me encourage you not to grow weary in well doing, for you WILL reap a great harvest if you do not faint.[1]

I know, for some, the last chapter's lesson might be a bit of a struggle. If you're used to living life by a long list of rules and then someone asks you to throw that list away and share a different way with you, it's not easy to embrace. But remember what I shared with you earlier regarding making changes in your life:

Change, even when it's for the better, is not easily received.

I admit, when God taught me I needed to "pray more, talk less, and focus on developing a *Godly conscience* within my children instead of my long list of rules," I struggled too…at first. I think my struggle was because I felt if I didn't have a lot of rules, I would lose control of my children, and I was absolutely right! I lost control, but God gained control. As a result, my children were able to transfer their "Godly conscience" living into all areas of their life, regardless of whether I was around or not.

Hopefully, you are able to apply the last chapter's **Put Into Practice** and begin to develop a consistent, daily prayer life for your children. Honestly, this was the greatest, most powerful lesson I learned in raising my children. My commitment to pray more and talk less kept me from destroying my relationship with them. Oh yes, instead of awakening their excellence, I could have very easily nagged my children right out of the house, filled with fear and insecurities.

But a dear friend named Trish Rowe, who has since gone to be with the Lord, gave me a book which challenged me to pray. It was a dainty, little pink book, but within its covers were verses from the Bible that could slay giants! Initially, I just *read over* some of the prayers, because…and can I keep it real…I really wasn't interested in praying! I only wanted results. At the time, I was recently divorced, and I felt like my children were confused, hurt, and unsettled. They began to express their bewilderment in various ways — all unpleasant! I found myself constantly emotional and physically tired, and I just wanted it all fixed! For the record, praying for my children was never foreign to me. I started praying for them years before I had even met their father. But the prayers I began during this time in our lives were different. Sometimes I felt as if I was on the front line in battle, while other times I felt like I was the reason for the battle. So, I had to take authority over what I could not see — over attitudes, desires, and persuasions. Those of you who have younger children, just wait until their teenage years when core values are challenged! I had to learn how to **sho'nuff** pray! But here's the lesson God wanted to teach me:

Through prayer I could believe, command, and declare it to be so.

So, I mustered up the faith to believe and I began to pray. It was over 25 years ago that I began daily to pray these verses faithfully over my children's lives, and I have continued to this very day. I began each verse with "God, I believe, confess and declare that…"

Sometimes what I was experiencing was far from what I was praying, but I kept on praying, commanding it to line up with the Word of God! As a result, I saw change. I saw the verses come to life in my children.

I would like to share the verses selected in my little pink book,[12] but before I do, I want to explain something. I was praying these verses when my children were going through temper tantrums, running away from home, battling with depression, having discipline problems, and more. So, this is not a "magical spell" that, once recited, makes your children become perfectly obedient. They are verses from God's Word, which I prayed in faith believing every single promise for my children. I believed that whatever I was experiencing right now was only a temporary state because

I expected God to fulfill every promise to the extent that my words confessed it, my emotions expressed it, and my actions confirmed it!

Over the past two decades, I have prayed these verses every day so they are no longer memorized but internalized. In other words, today when I pray, my heart rejoices. I get excited because I know God has accomplished and will continue to accomplish every single promise!

If you have been applying the previous "Put Into Practice" assignments, you have begun to develop a discipline of praying daily for your children. Here now,

---

12 Germaine Griffin Copeland, *Prayers That Avail Much for Women* (Special gift edition), Word Ministries.

I challenge you to build on that and begin praying this prayer of Bible verses, or one of your own, over your children. Do not be discouraged if you miss a few days or cannot complete the entire prayer every day. Start off small and build. What works for me is to pray at the beginning of the day, even before my feet hit the floor. It's a great start to my day and gets my mind in a place of gratitude and expectation. Below are several quotes from the book's prayer intertwined with additional verses that I have incorporated.

> ➢ Father, in the name of Jesus, I believe, confess, and declare Your Word over my children and surround them with my faith— faith in Your Word that You watch over it to perform it! (Jer. 1:12).

> ➢ I believe, confess, and declare that my children are Disciples of Christ, taught of the Lord and obedient to Your will. Great is the peace and undisturbed composure of my children because You God contend with that which contends with my children. (Isa. 54:13; 49:25).

> ➢ You care for them; give them safety and ease them. (I Pet.5:7).

> ➢ Father, You will perfect that which concerns me. (Psalm 138:8).

> ➢ Therefore, I commit and cast the care of my children once and for all over on You. They are in Your hands, and I am positively persuaded that You are able, and You will guard and keep that which I have committed unto You, for You are more than enough! (II Tim. 1:12).

- ➢ I believe, confess, and declare that my children obey their parents in the Lord, for this is right, and they live long, healthy, prosperous lives on this earth. (Eph. 6:1-3).

- ➢ I believe, confess, and declare that my children choose life! (Deut. 30:19-20).

- ➢ They love You, Lord, they hear and obey Your voice and cling only unto You, for You are their life and the length of their days. (Prov. 3:1-2; Deut. 30:19-20).

- ➢ Therefore, my children are the head and not the tail, they are above only and never beneath, they are blessed when they come in and when they go out. (Deut. 28:13, 3, 6). I believe, confess, and declare that You give Your angels charge over my children to accompany, defend, and preserve them in all their ways. (Psalms 91:11).

- ➢ You, Lord, are their refuge and fortress. (Psalms 91:2).

- ➢ You are their glory and the lifter of their heads. (Psalms 3:3).

- ➢ I believe, confess, and declare that my children are equally yoked. (II Cor. 6:14) in marriage with another believer in Christ, they love each other, are filled with the Spirit and they demonstrate the fruit of the Spirit daily. (Gal. 5:22).

- ➢ I believe, confess, and declare that their seed is mighty and from generation to generation they are saved, blessed, and highly favored. (Psalms 112:2).

- ➢ I believe, confess, and declare that I, as their mother, pray daily for them, love and encourage them, teach them honor and exercise wisdom in instructing them so as they grow older, they will not depart from the faith. (Eph. 6:4, Prov. 22:6).

- ➢ I believe, confess, and declare that I live a life of example before them. They see my good works and glorify You. (Matt. 5:16).

- ➢ I praise You, Father, because You are able to do exceedingly, abundantly more than I could ask or even think, according to the power that You placed within my children. (Eph. 3:20).

- ➢ The enemy is turned back from my children in the name of Jesus! (Psalms 9:3).

- ➢ I believe, confess, and declare that ____________ (insert your child's name) increase in wisdom and in favor with You God, and with man (Luke 2:52).

In Jesus Name, Amen.

PUT INTO PRACTICE

1. *Pray.* Continue the practice of praying every day for your children, even if it is only 30 seconds. It is truly a matter of life and death. Discipline yourself to be faithful in prayer.

2. Write down 5 to 7 qualities/attributes you desire your child's life to exemplify, not just for right now but also things for their future. For example, if you desire obedience, peace, wisdom, Christian marriage, and so on. Then begin meditating on your child possessing these godly traits.

Principle #6:
Build an environment that produces excellence

Chapter 10

A Lesson Learned from Popeye

I remember watching the famous cartoon character Popeye when I was growing up. He was a sailor who was an average guy with not much of a physique, except for his enormous forearms. He was madly in love with an equally average girl named Olive Oyl. Whenever she would fall into harm's way, Popeye would come to her rescue and every rescue required supernatural strength. But Popeye had no worries because he realized his strength lay in "spinach." So, before each rescue, he would consume a can of spinach and his strength was realized. I do not recall the very first episode of Popeye, so I cannot tell you how he came to realize his strength. I would like to think he had loving parents who saw how spinach awakened the potential within him, and they nurtured it by making spinach accessible to him.

Nevertheless, God brought to my mind the story of Popeye to teach me the following principle:

Awakening excellence is discovering your child's gifts, strengths, and talents, then making your home an environment where these qualities are nurtured and protected.

Of all the principles that God taught me in raising my child, this is the one that prompted me to write this book. So, let's look more closely at this principle because I can hardly wait to share with you what I learned. I will divide it up into two parts. First, we will discuss *"Awakening excellence is discovering your child's gifts, strengths, and talents."*

Parents have an awesome responsibility when it comes to raising their children. It can be overwhelming at times but nevertheless awesome. At some point during the journey of parenthood, we ask questions such as: Am I doing a good job? Am I pushing too hard? Am I not pushing enough? What activities do I involve them in? How am I going to pay for college? How am I going to keep the lights on? Ugh! All these stresses boiled down to the same question: How do I know what is the best for my child?

I think it's safe to say that every parent reading this book wants their children to succeed, but most of us feel like it's a gamble: Sometimes we win, but sometimes we lose. Wouldn't it be nice if all children were born with one set of instructions that work for each child? If we follow steps 1 through 12, then the finished product will be exactly like the picture. But this is not possible because each child is different. So, why do we try to raise our children with the "one size fits all" approach? We have seen, heard, or maybe even are one of those parents who did all the "right stuff." We made sure they took all the right college prep courses, put them in all the right extracurricular activities, help them learn an instrument or several languages. We even took them to church every Sunday, thinking they would be well rounded, get into the right college, marry the right person, and be successful. But oftentimes, it does not turn out that way. Then all you feel is tired, stressed out, and broken when your child tells you they need to take a few years off to discover themselves! How frustrating!

What if we did the "discovering" when they were young so they would not have to spend time, money, and energy discovering themselves once they are adults? This seems like such a simple discovery, but why is it that we as parents do the complete opposite? Once I discovered this, it revolutionized the way I raised my children. It was not about what I wanted them to be when they grew up (which is what most parents do), but it was about discovering their areas of excellence and then aligning them with the right environment that would enhance what they were already designed by God to do.

I meant well by forcing my oldest daughter to play softball. I kept saying to myself, "Good colleges want to see that you excel in several areas." But in all honesty, I should have explored other avenues because sports were not her strength.

And when I pushed and pushed her to perfect an area where she was weak, it only brought frustration, disappointment, and low self-esteem. As parents, we have to learn to work with discernment. We must use our eyes, ears, and heart to distinguish what is good from what is the best. Do you know how many hours we spent going to practices and games? Looking back, that time could have been better spent. I'll never forget the last game of the season; they were wrapping up their two-year losing streak. The batter struck out, and my daughter threw up both of her hands and said, "Praise God!"

I remember the coach looking at her and rolling his eyes, and her other teammates showed equal displeasure in her celebration. I must admit, that was not one of her finest moments, but it clearly exemplified to me how she was feeling. It transformed her usually gracious and sensitive demeanor into an obnoxious, insensitive person. At the end of the season, her level of skill, on a scale of 1 to 10, was still only about a 3. And there was no way that her coach/gym teacher/health teacher would be writing her a college recommendation letter.

One of the foundational scriptures that I had in raising my children is found in Proverbs 18:16. The International Standard Version states it this way: "A person's gift will open doors for him, bringing him access to important people."

Think of it this way: Let's say we've listed **your** strengths, talents, and gifts and assigned them points. The one you're really good at carries 10 points, but the one you are weakest at carries only 1 point. Most of us will focus on our weaknesses to try to bring them up. But what if, despite your best effort, the best you can do is increase by 3 points? After all your hard work and tears, you're basically in the same spot that you were.

Now, look at this same scenario in a different way. What if we forgot about everything else but focused on perfecting your gifts, bringing what you're already good at, to a level of excellence? Now **that** will open up some doors!

So, how do you recognize your child's gifts and strengths? First, don't be deceived into thinking that your child's gifts don't have to be nurtured, perfected, and protected, and we'll talk about that a little later. And please don't think that they will be wrapped in a pretty red bow and announce to you, "Here I am, the gift!" No, it may be quite the opposite. Every child has excellence within them. But sometimes it's covered up by attitudes, disobedience, anger, and all that comes with the stresses of life.

Let me explain. I remember one of my daughters, when she was very young, loved to take things apart. She would take apart the phone or dissect and inspect my bottles of seasonings, which was so frustrating to me because sometimes her fascination ended before she reassembled these objects! She was also very opinionated; she was the only child who dared to argue with me. Now you may say that's not a strength if she was getting into mischief and being disrespectful. Yes, on the surface, I would have to agree. But let's look deeper. What qualities, when nurtured, could be used in a positive, redeeming way? Remembe the disciple, Peter? He was very outspoken and hot tempered. Jesus could have very easily ignored or silenced Peter, but instead, he did just the opposite. At first glance, Peter's bluntness and temper seemed to be a negative quality, when nurtured, became boldness and zeal. Peter, along with James and John, became one of the key disciples. In the same vein, my daughter was showing me an area which, at the moment needed to be disciplined, but later would become a strength when nurtured. If you could have seen her when she was "researching" why an object worked the way it did, or "researching" what was beneath a wrapper and how it was put together, or seeing through her eyes her little mind deciphering as she was "building her case" for why she felt strongly about what she was discovering—then you would understand why I described these attributes as strengths.

Remember Popeye? I had to discover what the "spinach" was for my child. What does she possess that causes her to go from the average to the supernatural?

**Realize your child's strengths involve:
observing their actions, things they grasp quickly, things they gravitate to, things that cause them to get excited,
things they can talk about without you initiating the conversation.**

Do you know your child's strengths? What are you doing to build them up? Begin observing your child's behaviors, likes, dislikes. What do they gravitate to? Pray for discernment to discover their "bent" in life. Then, design a game plan for developing these areas. In essence, we're always discovering.

I had to *really* pray and ask for patience as well as discernment because, in the case with my daughter, I needed to know how to discipline wrong behavior without squashing her spirit. Remember, every child is different. God has given each of us strengths, so resist the temptation of trying to fit your child into a mold of **you** or making them live out **your** aspirations. Good intentions do not necessarily yield good results.

Remember when I said we will break up the principle into two parts? So, we will now examine making your home "an environment where your child's strengths are nurtured and protected"—but in the next chapter! For now, let's put into practice ways to discover your child's "spinach" and cheer them on.

Put Into Practice

1. Discover your child's gifts and strengths. This may involve making a list of the items I shared with you earlier (what they grasp quickly, what they gravitate to, what causes them to get excited, what they can talk about without you initiating the conversation). Begin thinking and praying about how you can nurture those strengths.

2. When you think you have uncovered a gift or strength, ask some probing questions to engage them further. Pick up age-appropriate books at the library on topics, activities, videos, or other ideas that spark their interest. Remember, the first phase to this is DISCOVERY, so keep your comments brief. You want to see if they engage.

Chapter 11

Let It Rain

Let's continue our current focus and discuss how *awakening excellence is realizing your child's gifts, strengths, and talents, then making your home an environment where their qualities are nurtured and protected.* In the last chapter, we discussed realizing your child's strengths, but in this chapter, I would like to share the lessons I learned about making your home an environment where your child's strengths are nurtured. God has given each of us a gift, but it is not stamped on our chest along with instructions when we are born.

My children's unique gifts were not automatically known to me. I had to pray, observe, interact, and then pray some more. But if you desire to aid your children in reaching their excellence, then—as I stated in the example I shared in the last chapter— you must find their "spinach" (or whatever awakens their excellence). However, you also need to place the can of spinach in their hands. Why? Because you are the parent. Remember from my introduction, the word *parent* means to bring forth. You are the one who must bring forth that gift, and nurture and protect it. I knew my children's gifts, talents, and strengths long before they even knew them. Ask yourself this question:

What can I make accessible to my children in order to cultivate their strengths?

You may think that you truly don't know your child's gifts, strengths, and talents. That's okay. I will share with you what I used to guide me. Notice the distinction I made in dividing up this principle into two parts: the first part is your child's *gifts*, while the other part is *strengths and talents*. There is an important reason for this: Spiritual gifts advance the church, but strengths and talents advance the world. Your child has both. I also believe that your child's strengths and talents are closely linked to their gifts, based on my study of Proverbs 18:16: "Gifts will bring you before Kings."

So, I started my discovery of my children's *gifts* first, and from there I realized their many strengths and talents. The Bible has many verses on spiritual gifts, but these are the ones I focused on: I Cor. 12:8-11; Ephesians 4:11-12; Romans 12:6-8; I Peter 4:10-11. I categorized them into three very general areas: Lead, Teach, and Help. Please hear me when I say this was my journey in discovering my children's gifts. You may take on a different approach, and that's perfectly fine. The important goal is that you take time to discover your children's gifts, strengths, and talents. You may research books, talk with people, take an online quiz (which I must add are numerous on the Internet and can aid you in discovering your child's gifts, strengths, and talents). But whatever road you take, just make sure that you remain prayerful and flexible. Do not put your child into a closed box when you determine what is and shall forever be their gift.

The next step is to observe your children and how they interact with their family unit, with people outside their family, and what helps them light up and shine. This is the fun part. I so enjoyed watching the way my children interacted, even when they were very young. Their little personalities would shimmer, and I thoroughly enjoyed seeing who they were becoming. I remember sharing with them how each snowflake that falls from the sky has its own identity, different from all the other snowflakes. That uniqueness was good. Often, we spend so much energy on expecting others to conform to what we want, but it can squash our individualism and deprive us of our creativity and sense of invention.

Also, do not be afraid to introduce new ideas and activities, and see how your children respond. You may not be a very artsy person, but perhaps your child Is. Introduce something that is even outside of your comfort zone. Keep in mind that it does not have to cost a lot of money. I remember my oldest daughter seemed to gravitate toward the sciences, so I found items from thrift stores and yard sales that related. I even asked several teachers at our local schools if they had science equipment they no longer needed. Soon, we had built a mini-laboratory in our home and we all enjoyed conducting various experiments.

After you have finished the first phase—prayer, study, observation, introduction—you are now ready to begin setting the environment that will nurture your children's gifts.

This is what I mean when I say we as parents must **nurture** our child's gifts. Let me share a story with you. Some may have visited or at least heard of Death Valley,[13] a national park in California (with a section located in Nevada). Nearly the entire park is wilderness yet has some of the hottest, driest regions in America. One record temperature was a scorching 134°F. On average, rainfall is less than 2 inches per year! It certainly lives up to its name because with these conditions one would **not expect** to see much life in Death Valley. Well, something phenomenal happened in the Spring of 1998. ***Conditions changed!*** Death Valley, known as a seemingly dried-up, unproductive land, was transformed into a beautiful blanket of wildflowers. What caused this amazing transformation? Rain! Not just the "usual 2 inches per year," but enough *consistent* rain to change the land's outcome.

When the environment changed, the land was able to achieve its ultimate potential!

Creating a nurturing environment for our children to grow also involves challenging them. For example, one day, I was speaking with my daughter—you know, the one who needed to take objects apart and discover how they worked. Well, one of her greatest strengths is research. There she was, at it again, taking apart something to figure out just how it worked. First, I had

13 Ask.com/wiki/Death_Valley_NationalPark

to check my emotions and discern which behavior was part of her strength versus her mischief. Then, a thought occurred to me. Instead of yelling to her about what clearly was a strength of hers, I would build an environment that challenged her to reach the next level. This is the same principle used in weightlifting or bodybuilding. Once someone has reached the next level of strength, what happens? You add more weight and increase the reps. This causes muscles previously unchallenged to be strengthened by increasing overall strength. As a result, I set out to discover what good learning toys and materials nurtured my daughter's strength. I found inexpensive radios, walkie-talkies, and clocks at yard sales and let her go at them.

My son was the opposite. He was a builder. Anything concerned with the construction of a building, he was all ears—the bigger, the better. He did the typical building projects: forts with chairs and blankets, LEGO blocks, popsicle sticks. But he was also fascinated with books on buildings. I remember when he was 3 and 4 years old, I brought him to the library and checked out books on architecture. We sat on the couch looking through book after book and talking about what fascinated him.

Creating an environment may mean contacting businesses and asking if your child can shadow someone for an afternoon. Whatever the gift, strength, and talent within your child, think outside the box for creative ways to awaken and nurture them. In the next chapter, we will talk about how you can **protect** your children's gifts, strengths, and talents.

PUT INTO PRACTICE

1. Discover your child's gifts, strengths, and talents. Remember to pray, study, observe, and introduce. Don't rush with this effort. It may take weeks or even months to know the uniqueness God created in them. But whatever the case, relax and enjoy the journey!

2. Let it rain in your home! Do one activity to create an environment that will nurture your child's gifts. Remember not to limit your choices to your own likes or preferences. Think outside the box, and you may discover some dormant talents of your own!

Chapter 12

10 Million Dollar Baby

Now to our final point in this principle: *protecting their gifts*. Reminisce on when you owned something priceless, something you truly loved to the point of wanting to protect it forever. In the same way, that is what we must do with our children. Their gifts must be protected, insured, safeguarded. Since we are their guardians (while they are young), that responsibility is ours. Why is it we spend more time and money protecting and insuring temporal objects instead of protecting and insuring our children's gifts?

What if I promised you, if raised properly, your child would make you a multi-millionaire? Would you change how you viewed them…
how you treated them….
how you protected them?

In raising my children, I noticed three main areas which I had to identify and guard my children against in order to protect their gifts. The first is easy to recognize: You must protect them from people and situations that can attack with the intention of **destroying** their gifts—namely, drugs, pornography, gangs, to name a few.

The older your child grows, the more challenging it will be to safeguard them from people and situations that clearly will destroy their gifts. Let me add it is easy to recognize what can destroy your child's gifts because such dangers usually have destructive consequences. They can destroy not only their present well-being but also impact their future. How do we combat these people and situations? I exercised two strategies: open communication and prayer! Children do not automatically know how to express their feelings in words, especially when faced with choosing between friends and family values. They need practice.

Yes, practice. They need to be taught how to respond in such situations. Just as you taught them how to tie their shoes, how to use the potty, how to learn their ABCs, your child needs you to teach them ways to respond to temptations. Open communication is vital. Your child has to trust you and know that what you are teaching is the truth.

The first lesson I taught my children was how to recognize potential trouble. Some situations can be avoided early in the game. I remember a girlfriend criticized me by saying that my children were too proper because they did not have, what she called "ghetto" friends. When I asked her what she meant by that she replied, "my son, can hang with those in the church and in the streets". I later thought: If that is how she chooses to raise her child, then no judgment from me. That's what she chooses to do. But my choice is to teach my children to assess situations, to choose to be around people of good moral character, and to avoid those whose "feet run to mischief" as Proverbs 6:18 says.

Why would I want my children to be friends with those who have a bad reputation or character and consistently make bad decisions. I have no desire to put my children in harm's way, nor is my goal to teach my child that hanging around those of bad reputation is making good choices. Proverbs 13:20 says bad company corrupts good morals. Thus, there must be another way to teach without placing my children in situations where their safety is mentally and physically challenged. But I was thankful to hear my friend's comment because it pushed me to pray for wisdom.

I made a decision to teach my children how to spot good character, how to recognize bad morals, how to exercise wisdom in choosing friends and places where they would go. I wanted my children not to be attracted to those of bad character; I also wanted them to discern when an environment is unhealthy so they would turn around and leave. This presented another challenge. While I wanted my kids to be uncomfortable in bad company so they would choose to leave, but I did not want to teach them to be judgmental. I speak more of this in later chapters, especially with writing a preamble for your children.

But what I did was expose my children to people and situations that differed from what they were accustomed to and then engaged in conversation about these differences. This involved traveling back to the city of my old neighborhood. I grew up in an area that is described as low-income/high-crime. When I drove my children through my neighborhood, I showed them the house where I grew up and spoke fondly about my neighbors. Our block consisted of families who were married couples with at least two children. There were husbands and wives who had parties once a month at home, with the men in the basement laughing, talking, drinking, and the women upstairs in the kitchen laughing, talking, and watching the kids playing outside. I would tell my children about the races we had in the street and how my father was so fast that he usually won most of the races. But then I told them about the "gangs" that would hang out in the alleys, smoking, skipping schools, getting high. We would see them with brown paper bags and wondered if they stole someone's ID to purchase alcohol. These were the guys who were up to "no good." I did this when my kids were young so they would understand early, but if your kids are older, I say it is better late than never. While riding through the neighborhood, I asked my children: Why did these gang members choose a different lifestyle than the kids I played with outdoors in my neighbor's yard? Why do people make bad choices? Are they bad people? Did they choose to follow others instead of leading the life they wanted? These questions evolved into good conversations about choices. How can my children choose not to get into situations? In the end, it is much easier to avoid a bad situation than to get out of one when you are in the middle of it.

It is very helpful for parents to share stories from their own life. Sometimes our children easily forget that their parents were once young and tempted to make bad choices. Sometimes they think we are immortal and perfect. I think it is important to let your children know you have made (and make!) mistakes, you did imperfect things and made bad choices, and you felt the repercussions of those choices—some of which may still impact you today. As a result, unbelievably, your child will start to look at you in a way that breeds trust because they know you are real and not just lecturing them about life. You yourself have experienced the best and the worst of life, and that is why you want the best for them.

Your children have to understand clearly and believe with all their hearts that you clearly love them and have their best interests in mind. You want them to seek out friendships that are in line with their family values and avoid relationships that are toxic. This is so important when they find themselves in tight situations because their family values must be the loudest voice in their heads.

Equally important, beware of those who will try to steal your child's gifts by consistently *hatin'* on your child. That is, there are individuals who will *not* blatantly try to destroy your child's potential, but they will plant seeds of insecurity, doubt, or jealousy that, **over time** will destroy or tarnish the excellence that is in your child. Haters come in all shapes and sizes. They may even be disguised as friends or even family members. Their seeds may take the form of a remark, an observation, or even a joke. They say something, then laugh about it, but it is still consistently hurtful.

Do not confuse this with constructive criticism; There will come a time when a person's comments on your child's character that may, at first, sound like a criticism, but in truth, they are observing a genuine character flaw which needs correction. Constructive criticism is welcome. Here, I am referring to remarks that involve name-calling, belittling, or targeting areas your child cannot change (emphasis on "things they cannot change.") These comments corrode your child's self-esteem, causing them to become timid and, ultimately, dumb-down their gifts, talents, and strengths.

Also, beware of those who make comments when your child begins to exercise an area of excellence—comments like "Can't you just act normal?" as if their definition of normalcy is something your child would even aspire to. These little digs will linger in your child's subconscious, and while they may not kill their gift, they will certainly redefine it. Children don't like sticking out or being labeled as different or weird. So they will hide their gifts in order to be accepted by their peers. as a parent, you must learn to multi-task. While teaching your child to avoid situations that will hurt their gift on one hand, you must also be strategic and intentional on the other hand to build up and celebrate your child's uniqueness. I like to call this teaching your kids to stand out, not stick out. It involves turning what society might deem abnormal or weird into what is uniquely special.

Let me illustrate this. My father was left-handed. When he went to school, every child was expected to use their right hand. Accommodations would not be made for anyone different, and those who rebelled were punished. The teacher would even use her yardstick and strike the left hand whenever the student used it as part of their normal process. Unfortunately, there was a stigma attached to those who were left-handed. It turns out both of my girls are left-handed, and for some very narrow-minded people, being left-handed is still stigmatized as abnormal and should be corrected. I totally disagree! Since I grew up hearing horrific stories surrounding those who were left-handed, I was on a mission! I found library books on left-handed individuals who made great discoveries, inventions, and contributions. If we were watching television or out in public and I saw someone left-handed, I made sure to point it out and discuss how special they were. Before my children started preschool, I spoke with the teacher, so she knew where I stood. I want to emphasize that I took the initiative to make sure they had desks that accommodated students who were left-handed. I spoke with the gym teacher, the music teacher, anyone who taught my children to insist on left-handed accommodations so my children would not be singled out and made to feel abnormal. Yes, I mentioned gym teachers because in our right-handed world, students are taught to play sports in a right-handed way. Once we visited Atlanta, Georgia, and I found a left-handed store—yes! Everything in the store was designed for those who were left-handed! We made a point of exploring the store and talking about what a special gift it was that they were left-handed.

The way to combat any threat to a child's gifts is to combat those who will try to destroy that gift. You must teach and build up. The lesson that God taught me was good parenting is not to roll in and take over a situation. Good parenting is teaching my children how to handle a situation.

Last, your child may need protection from themselves…yes, sometimes a child can be the biggest self-critic and feed themselves negative and destructive comments. Here is how God taught me to combat these negative influences. I had to view my children as He sees them. They are more than just **my** Million Dollar Babies! When I began to truly believe that statement, my actions reflected my views. Not only did I begin to view them in a new way, but I also taught them to view themselves similarly. They had to see their own potential. They had to view themselves as more valuable than millions of dollars.

I have shared with you that when my children were very young, I made it clear there were to be "no put-downs." They were not allowed to put each other down, and they were especially not allowed to put down themselves! When they were young, it was easier to protect their gifts because I, for the most part, controlled the environment. But as they entered school, I had to teach **them** to protect their gifts by not allowing themselves or others to abuse, disrespect, or tarnish their potential and who they were created to be.

Let your child know that it is also their responsibility to protect their potential.

This may be more challenging if your child is older. You may need to exercise patience and spend a lot of time building them up in order for them to realize they have potential. The word "potential" comes from the Latin *potentia,* meaning "power." Within every child is the power to change things for the better, but that power must be protected so that it can be allowed to grow and develop. Also, beware of labeling potential as *outward* beauty, for the very thing that others look at and say is weird or different may be an area of potential *within* your child. These put-me-downs, when repeated by others, can start to become real facts in your child's mind, even to the point that your child will repeat these negative comments on their own.

My parents moved in the middle of my junior year in high school. I switched from a predominantly Black student population to a predominantly White student population, where less than 1% were students of color. I felt this was very different because in my new school, no administrators or teachers looked like me. One day, in government class, while discussing the slave trade, my teacher said that Black people were sold into slavery because they were built like animals and were even said to have had tails. Then, the teacher looked at me and asked, "Pat, do you have a tail?" The whole class burst into laughter, but I sat, not knowing how to respond. I never told a soul that story until I was in my 50s—over 35 years later. The teacher said that within the first few weeks of attending the new school, but its negative impact stayed in my head and repeated itself until I graduated. While I was very active in sports and other extracurricular activities at my old school, this insensitive, racist comment made by the teacher at my new school stifled all of my desire to participate. I did absolutely nothing. I went to school, did my work, and came home. I wish I had had the confidence to stand up for myself, tell my parents, or at least prevent the teacher's comment from allowing me to enjoy my last year and a half of high school. But the bottom line is that I did not have the confidence to protect my potential, and it left me powerless.

I also want to mention that while there are many, more obvious killers of potential, such as drugs, alcohol, crime, violence, and so on, some are not so obvious as being killers, such as vulgar language, cigarette smoking, pornography, violent video games, and the like. build excellence and an environment so that their potential can be nurtured and developed wherever they go.

Your focus should be on building them up, so much so that when others say negative things—and they most definitely will—your child will have the power to speak up for themselves. They will dismiss negativity, be confident and self-assured. For example, my daughter experienced a similar situation as mine when she was in school. At that time, her father and I were going through a divorce which, needless to say, affected all of our children. Consequently, my daughter was not empowered at that time to stand up for herself nor did she show the confidence she needed to bring the situation out to our attention. Compare this to another situation when she was in school, and a teacher singled her out and verbally abused her. During this incident, I had put into practice many of the principles that I have shared with you. As a result, our family was in a much better place and, so was my daughter. She was confident in who she was therefore knew to handle the situation in a totally different way than before. She took the situation to one of the principals and shared it with me and her dad. We gave her the support she needed and let her know without hesitation that we would be at the school if necessary. What was the difference between these two scenarios? My daughter became empowered to protect her potential!

Parents, you cannot underestimate the confidence that comes when you build up your child.

Can you protect your child from every problem that happens to them? No. You cannot control other people's actions, period. But you can give your child every tool that they need to build resilience. Equip them so that when negative things appear, their potential will withstand and not be destroyed. They will not be deterred from achieving their excellence.

Chapter 1 emphasized that we are trainers. We teach, encourage, and exemplify what's right before God in a spirit of humility and expectation. As parents, we must guard against being overprotective, paranoid, and controlling. Our children belong to God...they're just on loan to us until they become adults. In another chapter, I will share my "preamble" to remember my responsibilities as a parent. But for now:

Put Into Practice

1. Begin a dialogue with your child, but keep it real…. Let them know everyone takes the necessary measures to protect what is important. Offer an example that they can understand. For example, explain how they would not wear brand-new sneakers to mow the grass or work in the garden after getting a French manicure! Why not? Because they see the potential of messing up, even destroying and losing, something of value to them.

2. Let your child know what a gift they are. They are your million-dollar baby, but not of monetary value! Point out how God sees them and what special qualities you see in them as well. Be genuine! Ask them if they understand how *priceless* they are and discuss ways they can protect their gifts. This is a good time to present various scenarios and to see if they found themselves in a challenging situation, how would they handle it? Remember, this is not a time to be judgmental. Think of your role as guiding and reminding them of what they have been taught so that they will be established.

Chapter 13

Go Team Go!

Back in the day, I used to be a cheerleader for the basketball team at Roosevelt Junior High School. We were the Rough Riders. Our team never won championships, but whether they won or lost, I cheered them on at every game with my whole heart. Whenever a member of our team stole the ball and scored, it didn't matter if we were behind or not. I remember our squad would simultaneously cheer, "Our team is red hot...*clap, clap*...Our team is red hot!" It wasn't so much that we *were* red hot and unstoppable, but we the Cheerleaders were hoping that our cheering would inspire them to play like they were. We knew that if we could inspire the team, we had a chance of winning.

As cheerleaders, our role was not to take the ball away and play the game for them.

It was to encourage, motivate, and build them up so *they realized* and *played* like they were winners, to the extent they had the will to fight even when the odds were stacked against them.

Learning to be your child's greatest cheerleader holds more power than you think. I mentioned in the last chapter that the very thing that others look at as sticking out in your child, could be the very same thing that allows them to stand out. Children tend to rise to the occasion, so if they feel their loved ones are in their corner cheering them on, then they strive to excel.

One of the most rewarding roles as a parent is to be your children's "cheerleader," the one who encourages versus the one who pressures or controls.

Let me share with you a lesson on the power of "cheering" that God taught me when my son was very young. My son was an exceptionally large baby—10 pounds—and, honestly, when the doctor showed him to me for the first time, he looked more like a toddler than a newborn! Well, as he grew, I started noticing that he had really large hands…. No, I'm not exaggerating; those jokers were *really* big! I knew, and those parents reading this book who have children with unique features can attest to this, that children can say cruel things. So, in my mind I was thinking, "Lord, am I going to have to fight somebody's mother because her child made fun of my son's hands?!" I cried out to the Lord and He said:

"You must learn to be your child's greatest cheerleader."

So, I encouraged my son by telling him what big strong hands he had and what great things he would do because of them. I would include his sisters by saying such statements as, "Go get your brother; he can help because he has big strong hands." Oftentimes, we would measure our hands, palm to palm, and I would say, "Wow, that's wonderful, your hands are almost as big as mine!" and he would smile and look so proud. He believed in his heart I loved his hands so much that if he thought I was sad or hurt, he would sit on my lap, cup his little hand, and place it on my cheek… and I would **always** smile. I hesitated about including this example in this chapter because I have never shared with my son the story behind my adoration for his "exceptional hands." But I feel it is okay to share it now that he's grown into them. Even at age 35, he still cups his hand and places it on my cheek…and I still smile! ♥

Yes, sometimes our child's uniqueness will cause them to not "fit in" physically or socially, and as a result, they feel bad about themselves. So, don't ignore your child's need for approval from you. Through the power of your words combined with actions that reinforce your words, you can turn that around. However, do not misunderstand me: I do not want you to lie to your child. Everything I told my son that I loved about his hands was true and heartfelt. Find one or two redeeming qualities about their *so-called flaw* and focus on the qualities instead of the flaw. Now, it may be they will still get teased and experience hurt, but at least they know in no uncertain terms that home is a safe place where they can feel good about themselves with people who love them and see the beauty in them.

I love the story of Dr. Temple Grandin.[14] She has autism. Temple didn't begin speaking until she was almost four years old, and the doctors who diagnosed her recommended she be institutionalized. I'm so glad her mother did not take the advice of the doctors for Temple went on to accomplish great deeds as a scientist. Temple admits she endured much ridicule growing up, but she continued to excel because of the undying encouragement and unwavering support of her mother and science teacher. Today, Temple is a leading advocate for the humane treatment of livestock and is the author of over 60 scientific papers on animal behavior. Her discoveries and inventions have revolutionized the slaughter of livestock. Over half the cattle in the United States and Canada are now handled with equipment she has designed for meat plants. Following her Ph.D. research on the effect of environmental enrichment on the behavior of pigs, she has published several hundred industry publications, book chapters, and technical papers on animal handling, plus 45 refereed journal articles in addition to seven books. She was named one of *TIME*'s 100 most influential people and even produced an award-winning documentary about her life. Pretty good for a gal who didn't speak until she was four, right? Temple's mother, Eustacia Grandin Cutler, talked about the struggles she experienced as she travelled on this journey with her daughter. She

14 https://www.appliedbehavioranalysisprograms.com

stated in an article published by the Autism Awareness Centre Inc (2016),[15] "There were no available therapy programs. Inclusion was not a word used by educators." Even through the mental and physical abuse by her husband Dick Grandin, Eustacia searched for good schools for Temple, looked for new therapies, fought for Temple's inclusion in neighborhood activities, and cheered her on to victory. Both Temple and her mother remain outspoken advocates in the autism community.

**She did everything within her power
to raise her daughter in an environment that
allowed her to
Stand Out,
not Stick Out.**

Notice above that cheering involves not only the use of words but also actions. While our words usher us in, our actions set the stage by lighting up the right environment for victory. When I cheered for my junior high school basketball team, even though we may have had fewer points than the opposing team, we didn't leave the gymnasium. We stayed and continued to cheer on our team. We also raised our pom-poms, pulled the crowd to their feet, and created an environment filled with high energy. These actions said: We believe you have what it takes to win, so we're willing to be here with you and invest our time and energy!

15 https://autismawarenesscentre.com/shop/parenting-family-1/personal-stories/a-thorn-in-my-pocket-temple-grandin-s-mother-tells-the-family-story/

You may be thinking: I see my child as average, so how do I cheer them on? Initially, I started cheering my children on in one area, but then it spread throughout everything they were involved in: church participation, school activities, their own decision making. Through this, I also realized how wonderful, interesting, and talented my children were; as I pondered how to encourage them, I kept finding more and more they could do. The result...I truly *became* their greatest cheerleader!

PUT INTO PRACTICE

Choose an area where you know your child is insecure. Practice encouraging them by looking at their insecurity in a different light. For example, find noteworthy persons who have "large hands," wear glasses, or have autism. Bring up their names and accomplishments in conversation and express how **you** respect or admire them. Remember, you are your children's greatest cheerleader. You possess what it takes to make them excel!

Principle #7:

Develop your Preamble

Chapter 14

Raising Your Child "On Purpose": The Preamble

Remember how when you were a kid, you would tell your mom when another child did something mean to you, like break your favorite toy, only for that child to say, "I didn't mean to." What was typically your rebuttal? I bet it was along the lines of "Uh-huh, they did it on purpose!" In essence, you were saying that the child had dishonorable intentions, and whatever they did to you was **planned** to harm you. Chances are, though, the child was not out to get you, nor had they spent hours devising some vicious plan. Instead, they broke your toy without giving it much thought.

How many of us have that same mindset when it comes to raising our children? Wouldn't it be nice if we raised our children **on purpose?** Most of us start out that way, paying attention to every detail of our child's life, charting every "adorably cute" thing they did in our baby journals, planning elaborate first birthday parties, spending money and time on something they will never remember. We've all been there! But because raising a child is an emotional task, we get burned out and, eventually, just start to *wing it!* I don't know of any parent who has been able to raise a child without sometimes **feeling** they were on an emotional roller coaster. Maybe that why it is sometimes difficult to be consistent when disciplining our children, since it's emotionally draining…we just don't *feel* like it. Then, when we don't feel like it, our child suffers because of our inconsistencies.

Most of us raise our children "on feelings" instead of "on purpose."

But here's the problem with that. In the a.m., we have such good intentions because we're energized, so we *feel* good about the decisions we make. We want our child to *feel* loved, our house to *feel* like a home. We want to *feel* like we're in control, even when we're not. But by the p.m., we're acting as if we don't see their disobedience because we're too tired to discipline them. For example, when they haven't completed their chores, we tend to use the cop-out line, "Just get out of the way…I'll do it myself!" Sound familiar? Therefore, I knew when it came to my children, I needed to focus on something besides my feelings to keep me on track. But how do I do that?… What's my motivation?

I had to take my eyes off of myself and put them on their future. Now I'm not talking about their immediate future, like next week when they are cleaning their rooms without me asking or taking out the trash before it overflows. I'm talking about their future as far as seeing them as adults. I imagine them being self-sufficient, making good decisions, and being kind-hearted to me as I age. I'm almost ashamed to admit this, but I even wrote out such an agreement on paper and tried to get my children to sign it! The agreement said that they promised to take care of me, be kind to me, talk nicely to me, and be supportive even when I was not pleasant. Of course, this would be carried out when I was older—much older! Needless to say, only one child loved me enough to sign this agreement!! So that is my example of what **not** to do.

But as always, after much prayer, I came to a better solution. It came to me during one of my many "exhausted moments." God prompted me to write a preamble. We usually think of the Preamble to the Constitution of the United States when we hear that word. It was necessary for me to write my own preamble down, because when I am faced with a task, especially one that is emotionally driven, a preamble helps me to stay focused throughout the process. But it couldn't be any old statement that "sounded good." It had to embody my purpose for staying motivated when I didn't *feel* like it. It had to be strong enough to take me out of my present emotions and catapult me into a place of focus and determination.

First, I spent time in prayer. Then I took a good, hard look at what I wanted to accomplish in the lives of my children. What did success look like? With the Holy Bible as *my* Constitution, I began writing a concise *preparatory statement* (not a book) of my goal in raising my children. It started with *We the People...* just kidding! I wrote my preamble this way:

To raise independent, God-fearing adults who are confident in making wise decisions, who have world vision and a non-judgmental love for people, and who utilize their gifts and talents to the glory of God.

It was brief and to the point, something I could recall and recite quickly. I then began to raise them "on purpose" with this statement as my goal. There is so much packed into this statement or preamble, so let's unpack it.

First, I had to remember that my job was to raise independent children, not children who were dependent on me to make every decision for them.

We tend to assume that when a young adult has a job, dresses nicely, drives a decent car, and has a secure place to live, they are independent. But don't confuse independence with the accumulation of *things.* I have experienced many adults who have so many things, but they are NOT independent because their parents provided it all for them! If you removed their parents from their life, these young adults would fall apart.

I'm an African American. Culturally, the African American mother (often referred to as *Big Mama*) is characterized as taking on the "I got this" role in the family. Big Mama raised the children and ran the household. She told us when it was time to eat, time to take a bath, and even time to go to the restroom. Whenever there was a problem, she knew how to fix it and always came to our rescue...as a matter of fact, she was proud of her role. It made her **feel** good about herself. Today, people would call Big Mama an enabler because, unlike the Chinese proverb,[16] she is *not* interested in teaching her little ones how to fish but prefers to fish for them. After all, why should they learn to fish when she's so good at not only fishing, but cleaning the fish, cooking the fish, and making sure they don't choke on the bones!

Knowing that *Big Mama blood* proudly runs through my veins, I had to separate my feelings of wanting to be needed, admired, and just plain busy from what I knew to be best for my children.

Don't mistake activity for productivity.

I could stay busy doing stuff for my children for hours, but was my "stuff" yielding the results that were best for them? Quite often, the answer was "no." I must confess this is **still** an area of struggle for me! When I get caught up in *busyness,* my children will remind me to calm down by affectionately referring to me as "Mommy Do Too Much!" How's that for a term of endearment?

That meant I had to step back on some things and allow my children to experience their ups and downs in life. God gave me a visual of the importance of raising my children to be independent. Imagine a baby, if you will, who is learning how to walk. The baby may take only a few steps before falling down. Now, what if every time the baby fell to the floor, I would run over and immediately pick her up, dry her tears, and put her back on their feet? That child would never

16 Ancient Proverb states, Give a man a fish and he will eat for a day but teach a man to fish and he will eat for a lifetime.

learn how to maneuver her body and learn to stand up on her own. Instead, she would fall down, then look up to me as if to say, "I fell down. Okay, it's time for you to pick me up!"

This may seem like a simple example, but often we as parents will fall into that same trap.

Sadly enough, this behavior will transfer to both teenage and adult life, and the grown-up babies will learn to whine, cry, and complain until you or someone else solves the problem and lifts them back on their feet. Worse yet, they will feel such behavior is acceptable as an adult and resent those who do not cater to their selfish, immature actions.

We have been fooled into thinking that we are being a "loving parent" when we rescue our children from every struggle they encounter. But can I keep it real? ...that's the attitude of an enabling, controlling parent! We rid our children of any type of struggle, we make every decision, and we control every outcome. Then, we get upset because they **expect** us to continue that treatment when they are adults. However, that's what we have trained them to become...dependent!

Struggles in life develop qualities in our child's character that are necessary to become a mature, independent adult.

Note to parents of young children: There will come a time when your child will be tested, and you won't be around to control the outcome. When your child experiences the pressures of life, wouldn't you like to feel confident that they have within them the discipline to persevere? Enabling them robs them of this quality. We must allow them to experience what I like to call "the toothpaste test."

You don't know what's truly inside of a tube of toothpaste until you apply pressure.

Some qualities will only develop under pressure, but please don't misinterpret what I am sharing. I am NOT saying you should abandon your child when they are experiencing struggle, not by any means! What I am saying is this: The way you responded to their problems when they were five years old should **not** be the same way you respond when they are fifteen or twenty-five. Yes, when they are very young, we have to make all the decisions, but when they begin school, we should slowly start **teaching them** how to reason, correctly think through options, make sacrifices to reach their desired goal, and so on. Practicing sound decision-making while they are young may also mean that some mistakes will be made…but you will help them by teaching, not enabling. With God's help, the end result will be independent mature adults who are confident in who they are and Whose they are.

The next part of the preamble states, "to raise God-fearing adults who are confident in making wise decisions." There were two intentional tasks that I had my children complete in order to fulfill this goal. The first and most important was to have them study the Book of Proverbs in the Bible. If you have not done so, please do. The Book of Proverbs is filled with teaching on wisdom, admonishment on wisdom, words of wisdom, and benefits of wisdom. I not only study the Book of Proverbs, but I had my children study it as well. As a side note, before they went away to college, I encourage them to read through the Book of Proverbs once again. I also wanted to make sure that I put them in the company of people who were wise—people who exercise prudence and wisdom.

The next part of the preamble talks about having World Vision. I felt this was important because we live in a huge world filled with people from all cultures. No one is exactly alike, but that is good! I wanted my children to be aware of that. Since my income was very limited, I had to be creative and develop a World Vision in my children's lives. So the second intentional task that I had them complete was found in the library. I had them research different styles of music and dance, which I love, and different types of food as well. I also took advantage of opportunities in which I was involved. For example, I was the Brownie Troop leader when my daughters were young, and we had an opportunity to put on a production, so I chose to do a program on international countries. As my children grew older, they had many opportunities to travel internationally. During the summer months, they would travel internationally with their father for work. Now I admit that is a little unusual, but I feel that was all part of an answered prayer to develop this World Vision in my children's lives.

Having a World Vision also resonates with the part of the preamble that states that children are to be non-judgmental. I wanted them to appreciate people who are different and to learn from them. I remember telling my children when they were very young that if you remain open-minded, you can even learn something from the homeless man on the corner, the least of which should be compassion. Finally, I wanted to make sure that my children realized that their gifts and talents were not given to them for arrogant self-glory, but to be a light that reflects God's love for the world.

PUT INTO PRACTICE

1. Pray. Then write a foundational statement that reflects your goal in raising your child.

2. Review it after a week or month to see if it still encompasses your heart's desire. If not, tweak it, and then live it…on purpose!

3. Ask yourself these questions to see if you are acting as an enabler. Do you feel that you are the only one who can assist your child through a problem? Do you make your child feel guilty for not sharing all their problems with you? When your child goes through a struggle, do you immediately take over and solve the problem without involving them in the decision-making process? If you answered yes to any of these questions…you just might be an enabler!

Principle #8:

Beware of controlling relationships

Chapter 15

Bon Appétit!

As I mentioned in my Introduction, the notes for this book are comprised of events I wrote about decades ago. It was a summer day, more than a decade ago, when I wrote this.

I love the summer for many reasons. The days are longer and filled with sunshine, giving me energy to find even more things to pack into my day and this summer has been no exception. Some wonderful things have taken up my time this summer. First, one of my daughters is home from college with me for the entire summer (yippee!); second, my son was selected by his university to participate in a special two-week summer project in Saudi Arabia (yikes!); and lastly, I met with a publisher to discuss turning my notes into a book (OMG!)

WOW! Can you believe I wrote this almost two decades ago?! I think I get the award for being the world's biggest procrastinator! But this is the classic example of how life gets in the way, and whatever you may feel is very important sometimes will get pushed back so far away that it's almost impossible to get it back. That's why the subject of this chapter is so important.

Make the time to have regular meals with your child a priority. Don't put it off! There's a cliché that says, "Time flies when you're having fun!" Well, I think time moves by faster as you age. I look back on the times when my kids were growing up and I think, wow, these past ten years have gone by in the blink of an eye. So, I encourage you to make the sacrifices, when your kids are young, to build solid relationships with them, encourage them even in small ways, and let them know they are unconditionally loved. You will never regret it.

But why, then, do we tend to procrastinate? One reason is that we don't see an immediate return on our investment. We live in a world of immediate gratification and "to-do" lists that are longer than my arm. So, when someone, like me, comes along and says STOP, make it a priority to have dinner with your child on a regular basis. This is important. Because we come up with a million reasons why we can't. So, I will share with you a simple habit that I used in raising my children that proved to be priceless. It all starts at the dinner table.

I've always loved summertime. When my children were small, it was a time of letting my hair down. We did not take many family vacations during the summer, but boy! did we vacation at home. There's even a term to describe it—a "stay-cation." It was always a time of bonding filled with fun activities. Now let me qualify that when I say fun activities: I don't mean running here and there because that can be stressful, but it was a time of creativity where our activities most of the time were spontaneous. My kids grew up in a neighborhood that had a wonderful sense of community. There were lots of families and several stay-at-home parents who were equally excited about the summer months. Even as my children grew older, the summertime still became a time of relaxation and fun activities. I remember one summer when I lived in a very small two-bedroom apartment; we were pretty much living on top of each other. However, we had a fantastic time just hanging out. One day, I invited a lady over for lunch, and she shared that her child was coming home for the summer too, but it was bittersweet. She shared that although she dearly loved her child, she didn't really "like" her child.

This got me to thinking…what caused me to "like" my children so much? Was it because we all enjoy traveling or watching movies together? Could it be that we are very competitive and challenge each other in board games? Or maybe it's because we all love to laugh? The more I thought about it, I saw that those were the "results" of liking my children, not the "reasons" I like them. When it comes down to it, I think the reason we enjoy each other so much is because we learned the art of being a family who shares similar convictions and respects each other's opinions, even if they differ. And this all began at our dinner table. Let me explain.

When my children were young, every evening I would have them set the dinner table. We had the dinner plate in the center, spoon and knife on one side, forks on the other, napkins folded, and glass placed at the tip of the knife.

I had a saying that my children heard throughout their childhood which was, "There are three times when I won't tolerate playing around…" and one of those times was at the dinner table. My reason? Dinner time should be a relaxed, enjoyable time for everyone, including me. I didn't want to have to discipline or correct my kids (nor did I want to administer the Heimlich maneuver!). Even though meals at the Dawkins household were nothing special (although sometimes we did eat off the fine china simply for the heck of it), but the atmosphere was very special.

Even when my children were in elementary school, dinner time was not a time where I did all the planning of the meals, fixing the dinner, setting the table, putting the food away, and cleaning up the kitchen. Note to parents: Just typing this makes me exhausted, so do not try to do all of this on your own if it does not bring you joy. Now, for those who were raised by Old School traditions, where the mom is the one who does it all: If it does not bring you joy, LET IT GO! Know your limitations. Why are you setting yourself up to be exhausted and frustrated with your family, because you chose to have all the responsibility on you? If you work outside your home and walk in the door tired, fixing dinner every night may become more like a second job rather than a pleasant experience. So, stop feeling guilty and ask for help. I've spoken with countless women who shared that they feel their family is ungrateful and selfish because they do not show appreciation for all the hard work that they are doing for them. I understand.

So, here's what I did. I came up with the menu for four nights during the week and, then, since I have three children, I had them each to plan a meal for one day during the week. Of course, I had to have some stipulations around the meal. For example, my son loves peanut butter and jelly sandwiches (even today at the age of 35, he eats a peanut butter and jelly sandwich pretty much every day). So, one stipulation was that the meal had to be balanced. And it had to be something they could fix with little or no assistance from me. So, in answer to what you may be thinking: Yes, my children planned the meal, but they also had to prepare it. Now, before preparation, someone had to buy the groceries, so I shared that responsibility with them as well, which turned out to be such a great learning experience. This all fit in to my preamble "to raise independent children who could make good decisions." We would plan a day to go grocery shopping to purchase the meals for the week. Now, I have to admit that once my children entered high school, it was very difficult to accomplish this task but nevertheless it lasted long enough for them to learn and appreciate all the time and energy that went into a family dinner.

Remember, you are the trainer, so use my experience as a springboard to what works well for your family. The litmus test that I use to determine whether I need to rethink my activity is twofold: One, does it fit into fulfilling the preamble? Two, am I able to serve my family from a place of love and joy? If the answer is no, for whatever reason, then restructure and ask for help. Do not set yourself up for failure. Learn to be flexible and do what's best for your family. I have a very close friend who does not like to cook. Her husband knew that before they were married, and her child knew that as well. So, did she pick up takeout every night? No. Sometimes she would, but they had family dinner time most nights at her mother-in-law's home. Now don't judge her, because it worked! Her husband and daughter were happy, her mother-in-law was happy, and my friend was happy, so it was a win-win. Regardless of who owns the dinner table, it is a wonderful place to build strong relationships, and you don't have to fix dinner every night to do that. Whether you divide up the responsibility among family members or eat at your mother-in-law's place, make it a priority to consistently dine together as a family.

After I learned this lesson, this is how I would now describe our dinner time. It was a time we focused on connecting as a family. We prayed together, shared, listened, encouraged, and planned activities with each other. There were definitely instances when someone was not pleased with another member of the family prior to dinner, but somehow, before the meal was even finished, the unhappy feelings were miraculously resolved and we would end up laughing with each other. As time went on, I noticed something even more important:

Dinner time became less of a ritual and more of a relationship builder.

We learned what was going on in each other's lives. We learned to support each other through the sharing of ideas and participation. Most of all, we learned to be a family. Some of our best family ideas were birthed at the dinner table.

I must admit that as the children entered junior high school and took on extracurricular activities, it became more challenging to spend hours at the dinner table every night, but we managed with shorter weekday dinners and longer weekend and summer meals. Thus, when summer came around, it was as though dinnertime together ushered in evening activities like board games, story time, or movie night.

Another idea that involves family time at the dinner table was our birthday dinners. This idea had a much greater blessing than I originally anticipated. I never threw big elaborate parties for my children growing up to celebrate their birthdays. I am not opposed to others having large birthday celebrations, but that was not what I chose to do. But I did plan birthday dinners for my children. Whoever had a birthday to celebrate, the honoree would plan their birthday menu and could invite one or two special people to enjoy the meal with the family. Now this was more like a fancy dinner party because we would use the good China and linen tablecloths and napkins, and we would decorate the honoree's chair. When their special guests arrived, they sat at the table with the family, and we would light the candles on the birthday cake. The honoree would be escorted in from a separate room to hear us singing "Happy Birthday." The best part of this birthday dinner celebration happened after the meal—and, no, it was not slicing the cake.

After the meal, as we sat around the table, each person was given a chance to say something special about why they appreciated the honoree. When I initiated this family tradition, the song that led me to do this was James Cleveland's "Give Me My Flowers While I Can See Them." The lyrics talked about how we too often wait until a person passes away to say wonderful things about them, but at that point they cannot hear or enjoy the beauty of those words. So, why not share why we love, respect, and appreciate another person while they are here on earth? This family tradition started more than thirty-five years ago when my first-born daughter was around three years old. I remember we lived in Chicago at the time. One of the young men in the ministry, Anthony, came over weekly to have Bible study and fellowship with my husband. He played games with my daughter and seemed genuinely excited about all of the fascinating toys in her toy chest. So, when it came time for her to choose her one special friend to invite to her birthday dinner, of course she chose Anthony.

To this day, we still have our birthday dinners and, yes, they are as priceless as they were thirty-five years ago. Even now, as adults, when we're all home, someone will automatically start setting the table and we pick right up where we left off. You may wonder how this *awakens the excellence in your child*. I challenge you to **Put Into Practice** having dinner together as a family. Then, after a month or two, I know you'll have the answer.

Bon Appétit!

PUT INTO PRACTICE

Have family dinner together. It doesn't have to be formal, unless you want it to be. Don't leave stimulating conversation to chance. Have a few, non-controversial topics ready to discuss. Remember, dinner should be fun and relaxing (not a time for correction or judgement). Let the family know well in advance when you plan to have dinner together. Make it engaging and special.

Chapter 16

Relationships

In my last chapter, I talked about "family time" and encouraged you to have dinner together. Let's continue our discussion and explore the family a little closer. But let's look at the relationships that family members have with each other, and how these relationships serve to awaken the excellence within your child.

Did you know that the word *family* originally derived from the Latin word *famulus* meaning servant? That presents an interesting dynamic, for this might suggest that those who live together are servants to each other. Could it be that the more we serve those within our family, the more closely we resemble what a family should be?

I have to confess something to you. In writing this, I was thinking: Yeah, I understand the servant part because I feel like a servant a lot of the times. I serve my husband and my children, I serve on the PTA at my children's school, I serve in Sunday school and vacation Bible school at church. I serve, I serve, I serve! I often ask myself the question: Isn't it supposed to go both ways? When will the time come when someone will serve me? I am a part of the family, right? The same principle that we talked about in the last chapter carries through into this chapter as well. If you want something, you must be willing to make it known and make an investment! That is true in any relationship, whether relationships between family members or relationships outside of the home. We will look at both types of relationships.

Let's first discuss the relationships within your home. Life was not always "rosy" for us, but over the years I have developed a wonderful relationship with my children! So, what makes it wonderful…now? Is it because they are my children? Possibly. Is it because we have mutual respect for each other? That has much to do with it. Or is it because we're all such great people and everyone loves and wants to have a relationship with us? Maybe for my children, but not for me! I believe it's because my heart truly desires it and I am willing to invest in it. I confessed it daily and then put my *confessions to work!*

Now here's another confession: Oftentimes, I did not **feel** like working at our relationship.

While loving my children came naturally, building a good relationship required work!

When I say "work," I do **not** mean hard physical labor. I had to work on *changing my thinking.* And to change my thinking, I had to be willing to let go of "stuff." If I was wrong, I had to be willing to admit I was wrong, even if it was to my child.

Sometimes I don't feel like being the first one to apologize or change a bad behavior. Sometimes I just want to be left alone—indefinitely. But honestly, operating in my feelings is not what builds family. Decide what kind of relationship you want to have with your child. Is it a relationship that encourages or criticizes everything they do? Is it one that loves unconditionally or one that only loves *if* they act the way you want them to act? Is it one where you forgive or hold wrong over their heads to the point of forming a dark cloud? It's time to purge those bad attitudes and actions.

Yes, I had to purge. Some things had happened in the past that I had to be willing to release, forgive, and not bring back up. It's time to throw out those ill feelings we have been harboring against our children for what they did *months* ago, what they may have forgotten but we haven't forgiven. Please, heed this advice…it's time to get rid of old stuff from our past that we have placed on our children, things over which they had no control. Can I keep It real? ThIs means that if you don't like their daddy (or mama, grandma, sister, etc.), stop transferring your anger to your children. These issues have interfered with our parent-child relationships for too long…let's start fresh with our children and build on awakening their excellence.

It is detrimental to operate within a family if you are not willing to serve. Take it from me, you may not always feel like working at the relationship, but by living in the same house, there is a good chance you will cross each other's path. So work, even when you don't feel like it, because the reward is priceless. My grandparents lived by Eph. 4:26, "…don't let the sun go down on your wrath." Every night before they went to bed, they would kneel on the floor and pray together. My grandmother would pray out loud for my grandfather, and my grandfather would pray out loud for her. Any animosity they might have had for each other during the day was settled before they shut their eyes for the night.

Now let's talk about relationships outside the home. I know so many parents who raised their children as best they knew how, only to learn their child chose to hang out with the wrong crowd. Bad relationships can ruin your child's excellence to the point where your child's actions are unrecognizable to you. I grew up hearing these kinds of stories and even saw this among friends of mine, so in the back of my mind, I had the fear of what if my child got caught up in the wrong group or, worse, what if my child made a decision not only to jeopardize their future but the future of their friends? First, I had to deal with that fear. You cannot raise children of excellence when you are dealing with fear. I say this because fear paralyzes a person, fear causes paranoia, fear destroys trust and relationships. Choices always need to be made throughout life. Wherever you go and whatever you do, you will eventually have to decide to go to the right or to the left. After much prayer, I believe it was God who gave me one of the most impactful principles I have ever received. This final nugget for awakening the excellence within my children was:

The Principle of Voice and Choice

If your children are ever in a relationship where they do not have the freedom to voice their opinion or choose to do what they feel is important without the fear of verbal or physical abuse, then they are dealing with a controlling person and they **need to leave** that relationship...immediately. Let it go! Only after the controlling person has sought out professional help and your child has witnessed consistently changed behavior, then they may choose to revisit the relationship. Your child should never ever be in a relationship where, if they choose not to go along with the crowd, they will be badmouthed, insulted, rejected, ridiculed, or harmed. I remember when I worked at a high school, there was a young girl in tenth grade. I was in charge of organizing an after-school event that was open to the community and needed student volunteers. I encouraged the young lady, who was very artistic, and other students to volunteer a few hours after school to organize and help set up. To my surprise, she told me she would let me know if she could volunteer *after* she spoke with her boyfriend. Now the natural assumption was to think that she and her boyfriend had something planned after school and she wanted to respect that. But no, she told me they had nothing planned; her boyfriend just likes her to go straight home after school. Moreover, not only was she to go straight home but, when she got there, she was to go to her room and call him to let him know. Well, one of my eyebrows shot up because I was thinking: He wants you to do what? I asked if this was something she chose to do, or did she feel she would be harmed if she was not obedient to his demands? She smiled and said, "You don't want to know." I decided to report this conversation immediately and recommend her to the school counselor.

You may say that was a ridiculous situation. But don't judge this young lady too quickly; controlling relationships do not *start out* as blatantly controlling. There are no flashing lights around the person that warn "Avoid me! I'm controlling!" The relationships begin casually., Friends might describe them as "Love birds, they're *always* together". Or say, "She really *loves and cares* for him" and "Oh, look at how protective he is of her." It is also important not to take this to the extreme and think that every time someone wants to spend time with, protect, or care for your child, they are trying to control every move. Many healthy relationships involve two people who love, protect, and care for each other and enjoy each other's company all the time. When your child is blessed to be in one of these healthy relationships, you should be cheering them on. But let's look more deeply at what I'm referring to as a relationship with a controlling person.

For almost three decades, I have studied controlling relationships. I have talked with old and young. I've studied the traits of controlling persons, their behaviors, speech, and tendencies. There are signs of a detrimental controlling relationship, and there are also stages your child should be aware of so to detect whether they themselves are controlling or if they are getting involved in a relationship with a controlling person.

The first stage is isolation. Does this person try to isolate your child from their support system? In other words, do they try to either physically or mentally separate them from family and close friends? They may start by having your child questioning the motives of those who are closest to them or make requests like "IF you love me, you will break curfew and stay here with me." If your child does not comply, the person will do *reverse isolation* and stop responding to your child's texts or talking to them for a few days as a form of punishment. This is done until your child breaks down to demonstrate their loyalty to the controlling person.

The second stage is what I call break and rebuild. The controlling person begins tearing down or punishing your child for not complying with their wishes. This may start out with minor insults: "You're too fat…you're too skinny…you look ridiculous with short hair…. don't wear that pink shirt, that color looks bad on you…" The strategy is to break your child's spirit by restricting behaviors and using insults, name calling, or even physical abuse. Once broken, the controlling person can rebuild an insecure, dependent person over whom they have power. Recall the example I used earlier about the girl in high school. She was a very talented young lady with beautiful features and an above-average student. She just became victimized by a person who approached her with what she viewed as a demonstration of love but, over time, transitioned into a nightmare. Her partner's true identity was not revealed until she had, as she described, fallen in love with him. I should add that a person who is controlling usually looks for nice people. That is, they prey on those who have good hearts and good intentions; those who see the best in people and are generally described as sweet people. I guess that's because nice people are great insurance for those who wish to control—nice people ensure bullies will live long enough to move on to their next victim.

The final stage is guilt. When your child decides to end the relationship, the controlling person feels they will lose their control and begin with over-the-top apologies, sometimes crying, sometimes threatening. They will threaten to hurt themselves so your child feels guilty about leaving them. They make promises they usually do not keep for the long term, like starting counseling, not drinking anymore, and so on. They will say and do whatever it takes, short term, to keep your child under their control.

In helping your child recognize controlling relationships, you must maintain a sweet balance because you do not want to scare them away from relationships, but you want to educate, empower, and enlighten them to be aware and make wise choices. One of my goals in raising my children was to develop their character to a high standard, so they would seek out relationships with people who are like-minded. These are the relationships they would find attractive because they felt comfortable.

Studies have shown that most people act on how a situation makes them feel, not on whether it is the logical choice[17]. We make purchases, adopt bad habits, and will marry someone because of how it makes us *feel*. So, if your child recognizes a relationship that takes a turn from encouraging to controlling, they will not feel good about continuing in that relationship.

---

17 https://www.psychologytoday.com/us/blog/intense-emotions-and-strong-feelings/201101/like-it-or-not-emotions-will-drive-the-decisions

My prayer is that they will feel secure enough in their relationship with *you* to come and talk through it and get support, if needed, in exercising their voice and choice.

My desire is that the principles contained in this book will empower you to speak to the Trainer in you and command it to arise. Proverbs 23:7 (NKJV) states: as a man "thinks in his heart, so is he." Now I know this scripture, in context, is talking about how a stingy man, even though he tells you to eat, is always thinking about how much will it cost him in his heart. But this principle can also be applied here. Let me explain: I had to really work at being patient, kind, and even truthful. When I tried to *fake it,* my children could see right through that. Unlike that "stingy man," my desire to have a healthy relationship needed to be real and from the heart and not phony for when we were in public. You may not treasure having a good relationship with your children when they're young, but wait until they're older. A good relationship will save you from many woes.

Put Into Practice

Let's *Keep It Real.* Ask yourself: "Do I really **want** to have a good relationship with my child?

> ➢ If yes, great! Continue confessing it and find ways to *put your confessions to work.*

> ➢ If not, why not? Are you secretly angry with your child for something they can't control? Are you jealous of your child because they possess qualities you wish you had? Are you controlling? Did they do something to you that you haven't forgiven them for? Whatever it is, expose it and deal with it. You must deal with the root of the problem for the relationship to grow.

> ➢ Now let me encourage you: You're on the road to recovery, or else you wouldn't be reading this book.

PRINCIPLES

Principle #1: Live by example: *Desire to be the person you want your children to become, and watch God fine-tune your character through your children.*

Principle #2: Take control of your emotions: *Yelling keeps you and your child in a vicious defeated cycle. Teach your children to respond to "instruction," not "emotion." If your instructions are drowned out by emotional outbursts…the lesson is not learned. Therefore, the child's behavior will not change.*

Principle #3: Understand the power of your words: *Stop speaking what your children are and start speaking what you desire them to become.*

Principle #4: Pray more, talk less: *If you are truly committed to seeing a behavior change in your child, then you must talk to God about it twice as much as you talk to anyone else about it…including your child.*

Principle #5: Focus on Character not Rules: *To build children of excellence, you must focus on building godly character instead of a list of rules. Build conviction rather than rituals.*

Principle #6: Build an environment that produces excellence: *Awakening excellence is discovering your child's gifts, strengths, and talents, then making your home an environment where these qualities are nurtured and protected.*

Principle #7: Develop your mantra: *My focus is to raise independent, God-fearing adults who are confident in making wise decisions, who have world vision and non-judgmental love for people, and who utilize their gifts and talents to the glory of God.*

Principle #8: Beware of controlling relationships: *Healthy relationships allow each person to exercise their Voice and Choice without the fear of being harmed, verbally or physically .*

FOUNDATIONAL VERSES

➢ Keep putting into practice all you learned and received from me—everything you heard from me and saw me doing. Then the God of peace will be with you. (Philippians 4:9 NLT)

➢ Train a child in the way he should go, and when he is old, he will not turn from it. (Proverbs 22:6 KJV)

➢ Never stop praying. Be thankful in all circumstances, for this is God's will for you who belong to Christ Jesus. (I Thessalonians 5:17-18 NLT)

➢ I will teach all your children, and they will enjoy great peace. (Isaiah 54:13 NLT)

➢ Your towns and your fields will be blessed. Wherever you go and whatever you do, you will be blessed. (Deuteronomy. 28:3, 6 NLT)

➢ But the fruit of the Spirit is love, joy, peace, forbearance, kindness, goodness, faithfulness, gentleness, and self-control. Against such things there is no law. (Galatians 5:22-23 NIV)

➢ Praise the Lord! How joyful are those who fear the Lord and delight in obeying his commands.[2] Their children will be successful everywhere; an entire generation of godly people will be blessed. (Psalm 112: 1-2 NLT)

> ➢ The Lord Himself goes before you and will be with you; He will never leave you nor forsake you. Do not be afraid; do not be discouraged. (Deuteronomy 31:8 NIV)

About The Author

Patricia Dawkins

Educator, author, entrepreneur, and single mom. Patricia Dawkins has spent over 35 years in education, ranging from directing Christian education at her home church to teaching financial literacy to low-income adults to developing Black History Month programming for elementary schools. A native of Columbus, Ohio, she grew up in the 1960's, when everyone knew their neighbors, and children had to be home when the streetlights came on. She is a first-generation college goer and earned her BA in Communications at Ohio University and her MBA from Ohio Dominican University.

She has three children, Elise, Christina and Jonathan. And the newest member of the familyis JaLisa, Jonathan's wife, who she affectionately refers to as her "new daughter". This book is inspired by her journey raising her children.

Printed in the USA
CPSIA information can be obtained
at www.ICGtesting.com
CBHW021648191223
2691CB00004B/15